CONDITIONS
MAY VARY
A Guide to Maine Weather

Gregory A. Zielinski

To Ann, Chris, Catie, and Andy

and to the hardy souls of Maine who endure
and relish the state's weather and climate

Copyright © 2009 by Gregory A. Zielinski

All rights reserved.

ISBN 978-0-89272-696-7

Cover photograph: INFO TK

Design by Chad Hughes and Lynda Chilton

Printed at Versa Press, East Peoria, Illinois

5   4   3   2   1

Library of Congress Cataloging-in-Publication Data available on request

BOOKS·MAGAZINE·ONLINE
www.downeast.com

Distributed to the trade by
National Book Network

TABLE OF CONTENTS

ACKNOWLEDGMENTS

There have been many individuals who have helped make this book possible. Foremost I want to thank the editors of Down East Books (Michael Steere and initially Neale Sweet) for their belief that the individuals of Maine, visitors to the state, and overall weather maniacs, would be very eager to read about Maine's weather and climate.

I want to thank members of the National Climatic Data Center and other state climatologists for their assistance in obtaining and evaluating climatic data for the state while I was the State Climatologist. In particular, I am so thankful to Barry Keim, now Louisiana State Climatologist, for his assistance in obtaining climatic data as well as his friendship. Members of the two National Weather Service Forecast Offices in Maine (Caribou and Gray) were very helpful in discussions on particular climatic and weather events around the state over time including Albert Wheeler, Meteorologist in Charge at the Gray office and contributor to the book, and Daniel Cobb, formerly of the Caribou office. A very special thanks and appreciation goes to Hendricus Lulofs, Meteorologist in Charge of the Caribou office and contributor, for supplying me with many, many pieces of information and images that are used in this book and to John Jensenius of the Gray NWS office for the many photos of specific weather events from around the state.

Thanks also to Darrin Figursky, Meteorologist in Charge of the Raleigh, NC, NWS office for providing me with sources of information I used in the book. I especially want to thank members of the Climate Change Institute at the University of Maine, particularly Paul Mayewski, Director, for their support when I was the Maine State Climatologist and a research professor at the University. Funding for various studies on the past weather and climate of New England was provided by the Paleoclimatology Program and the National Science Foundation, thus they contributed to this overall effort. Neal Pettigrew, GoMoos Chief Scientist and UMaine Department of Marine Sciences, contributed several photos and provided useful information on the nature of currents and the buoy system in the Gulf of Maine. Others have contributed photos I've used, such as Catherine Schmitt and William Sneed, and I am most grateful. I am especially grateful to Bill Larrabee, observer at the Sebec Lake Co-Op Weather Station, for photographs he provided and friendship when I was the State Climatologist. My apologies to anyone that I have forgotten to mention by name.

Most of all I want to acknowledge my family for their ongoing support and assistance in so many of my endeavors related to this book and beyond. Most of all, I am so grateful to my wife Ann. Not only has she been supportive of my work, but her abilities and artistic eye were invaluable in getting many of the figures compiled and in good form for this book. I also thank my children, Chris, Catie, and Andy for their support in all of my work especially when I no doubt took time away from things they needed to have done. In this case, I am especially thankful to photos they contributed to the book as their love for the outdoors of Maine clearly comes through in their interests. I also thank my father, Zigmond, and my mother, Doris, for their efforts in raising me as I would not have gotten this far without them.

1

THE CULTURE OF MAINE'S WEATHER

Maine is a state known for its rocky coastline, its lobsters and blueberries, and for the fun that its ocean and mountains bring to tourists and Mainers alike. It is also known for its people, their independence and fortitude. Maine is "Vacationland," as prominently displayed on one of the state's license plates. Its more official nickname is "The Pine Tree State," and given that 90% of the state is forested, the highest percentage in the United States, this is certainly a valid nickname. Maine is also known for its weather, probably most of all for its cold winters and snowstorms. Those may be icons for the state, but there are many other weather types dictating the interactions between people and Maine's natural environment. The weather of Maine is dynamic and can be so unpredictable that Mainers can easily be said to have adopted it as an icon for their lifestyle. You have only to read the description of the weather event detailed below for a clear, and humorous, example of what Mainers must cope with.

■ AN UNEXPECTED TURN OF EVENTS

As the end of March 1992 approached, many Mainers were undoubtedly looking forward to spring-like weather, getting their tomato plants started inside, and possibly getting ready to start spring cleaning. Temperatures had not only risen to 50°F in Portland several times in early March that year, but also in the last few weeks of February. There had not been a measurable snowfall in Portland since the end of January and by the end of March the ground had no snow cover. Kennebunkport had a high of 58°F on March 6 and Sanford had four days above 50°F in early March, including a high of 58°F on the 5th. Many people in southern Maine were probably thinking of an early spring, and the weather forecasts were not indicating anything very different from this progression out of winter. But the notorious and often unpredictable weather of Maine was about to throw a major-league curve ball. At 9:17 PM on Thursday, March 19, the National Weather Service issued the following forecast for the midcoast and southwest coasts of Maine.

> **Tonight:** Mostly clear. Lows near 20. Northeast wind around 10 mph. Some minor coastal flooding possible at the time of high tide near midnight.
>
> **Friday:** Partly sunny. Highs in the mid to upper 30s. Light wind.
>
> **Friday night:** Mostly clear. Lows in the teens.
>
> **Saturday:** Mostly sunny. Highs 30 to 35.

This was not the kind of forecast that would make someone pay serious attention to the weather for the upcoming weekend. Not much had changed by early Friday morning. The forecast released at 3:04 AM indicated that a fairly nice couple of days lay ahead for the midcoast and southwest coastal areas. Twelve hours later (3:01 PM, Friday, March 20) computer models produced the same forecast for the southern coastal regions. By Friday evening, a small change in the forecast occurred. There was now a chance of flurries; however, this was just a minor change and there still was probably very little concern about weather conditions over the next few days. At 9:23 PM on Friday, the forecast called for a 30% chance of flurries, but atmospheric conditions were changing. Here is the forecast that was issued at 9:23 that evening.

> **Tonight:** Variable clouds with a 30 percent chance of flurries. Lows 20 to 25. Southeast winds 5 to 10 mph becoming variable. Minor flooding possible along the coast around midnight due to high tides.
>
> **Saturday:** Becoming sunny. Highs around 30. Northwest winds 5 to 15 mph.
>
> **Saturday night:** Mostly clear. Lows in the teens.
>
> **Sunday:** Sunny, then clouds increasing during the afternoon. Highs around 30.

By midnight on Saturday, the stage was set for Maine's weather to show its unpredictable nature. In other words, the fun was beginning. It started to snow along the southwest coast around midnight Saturday. In some areas, the snow began to fall at the rate of 3 to 4 inches per hour, and the game of "catch-up" began. This meant that the forecasts for early Saturday morning were essentially only accommodating the amount of snow that had already fallen. The next forecast for the midcoast and southern Maine, released at 1:07 AM on the 21st, was as follows.

> **Tonight:** Snow ending, then partial clearing. Accumulations 1 to 3 inches with some patchy accumulations near 4 inches. Lows 20 to 25. Southeast winds 5 to 10 mph becoming variable.
>
> **Saturday:** Becoming sunny. Highs near 30. Northwest winds 5 to 15 mph.
>
> **Saturday night:** Mostly clear. Lows in the teens.
>
> **Sunday:** Sunny, then increasing clouds in the afternoon. Highs near 30.

Yet, as of early Saturday morning, some areas along the southern coast already had 4 to 8 inches on the ground. This prompted the following forecast at 3:37 AM for the southwest coast.

> **Snow advisory early this morning.**
>
> **Today:** Snow ending this morning, then becoming mostly sunny. Total accumulation 4 to 8 inches. High in the mid-30s. Winds becoming northwest, 5 to 15 mph.

As dawn approached on Saturday, the forecast released at 4:54 AM emphasized potential snowfall amounts along the southwest coast. Interestingly, even this late in the event, the computer forecast models did not calculate the magnitude of the situation successfully.

> **Winter storm warning early this morning.**
>
> **Today:** Snow ending this morning, then becoming mostly sunny. Total accumulation 6 to 10 inches except 10 to 15 inches in the vicinity of Portland. Highs in the mid-30s. Winds becoming northwest 5 to 15 mph.

Finally by mid-afternoon, the snow began to diminish and eventually stopped late in the day on Saturday. The 30% chance of flurries forecasted at 9:00 PM on Friday ultimately produced snowfall totals well over 10 inches along the southwest coast of Maine, with an unofficial snowfall of 30 inches at Goose Rocks Beach in York County. The weather phenomenon that produced this "surprise snowstorm" is referred to as a NORLUN Instability Trough. It is not a distinct low-pressure or storm center, but results from a group of conditions that can form along the Maine coast. This type of weather features a persistent flow of air off of the ocean that helps to produce the 3-4 inch/hour snowfall rates and ultimately the high snowfall totals. Computer models in the early 1990s were not able to predict this kind of weather event very well and, according to Hendricus Lulofs of the Caribou National Weather Service office, the more refined and intricate models of today are still unable to consistently predict their occurrence, nor are they able to reliably predict where the highest snowfall rates will occur. Truly the NORLUN Instability Trough is a great example of the complicated nature of Maine's weather.

■ THE FORTITUDE OF MAINERS: THE EARLY DAYS

Mainers are hearty souls, willing to withstand deep snow, blizzards, and cold temperatures, particularly when these conditions are unexpected. In fact, winter-like conditions may exist in certain parts of the state at any time during nine months of the year. On the other hand, summers can have temperatures in the 90°Fs with high humidity and torrential rains. In fact, both drought and wet spells with the possibility of flooding may occur frequently within the same year. Hurricanes and all levels of tropical systems can have a direct impact on the state and even tornadoes may occur along with very severe thunderstorms. There is no shortage of weather types and events to challenge the fortitude of Mainers. This is especially true as so many individuals are dependent on the weather, such as farmers, fishermen, foresters, and those in the tourist and recreation industries. Public works departments are also highly cognizant of approaching weather systems, especially once the dreaded "winter weather advisory" or "winter storm watch" is issued by the National Weather Service.

It is noteworthy that the perseverance of individuals in the face of Maine's weather is not something that has come into existence over the last century. It is true that our dependency on modern technology makes us more susceptible to the fury of a severe weather event than were early settlers with their more-simple lifestyle. This is especially true of modern travel and communications. However, the first Europeans who settled here had fewer conveniences to help protect them from the weather as a whole, and particularly, from the different types of storms that move into or form in the state.

An example of the adversity past Mainers endured from the weather occurred during the summer of 1816. That year is commonly referred to as the "Year Without a Summer," as well as "Eighteen Hundred and Froze to Death," ominous descriptions no matter which is used. Snow was recorded in June just about everywhere in Maine that summer, and accounts of conditions in July by Stommel and Stommel (1983) include "ice froze as thick as window glass" on July 5. Of even greater significance to settlers was the frost on July 9 that again killed much of the corn crop in the state except in the most sheltered areas. Corn in Warren was cut down by the frost on this day as it was just hoed for the first time. Professor Parker Cleveland at Bowdoin College recorded a temperature of 33°F on the morning of July 9 and frost was reported in many places around Brunswick. The cool nights were very unfavorable for vigorous corn growth and failure of the crop was certain throughout Maine and New England as a whole. In fact, the Portland publication *Argus* advised farmers on July 17 to plow their grasses under again and resow for new growth to appear by the end of summer. The poor growing season in 1816 also led to an increase to 75 cents per bushel of potatoes—up from the usual price of 40 cents per bushel. Such conditions would be quite traumatic for today's farmers, but think of what it meant to the farmers of 1816 who were so dependent on their crops for survival.

Unfortunately, the poor weather in the summer of 1816 was the turning point in the future of many people in Maine. The size of many farm families was large, thereby preventing many sons from inheriting the family farm. In addition, the amount of available land suitable for agriculture in Maine at this time was very limited. As a result, many young people were probably contemplating a westward emigration to find new land in the fertile farmlands of the central part of the country. In particular, those who had previously moved to the areas around the Ohio and Mississippi Rivers encouraged their siblings to move out of Maine and northern New England, as a whole. The bad crop of 1816 was enough to convince many to emigrate westward. Many sold their farms in Maine, with some of the poorer farmers leaving on foot for Indiana and Ohio. Clarence Day, in his book *History of Maine Agriculture*, referred to one such family of eight who walked from Maine to Easton, Pennsylvania, dragging their possessions behind them. He also noted a single day when a train of 16 wagons with 120 men, women, and children left Durham, Maine, passing through Haverhill, Massachusetts, en-route westward to Indiana. Although not the sole reason for this migration out of Maine in the early 1800s, the weather and climate of the time played a significant role in the process.

The weather and climate of Maine also played a key role in the American Revolution. Benedict Arnold led his troops on the Quebec Expedition during the fall of 1775 from Fort Warren, Augusta, through the hills of west-central Maine to Point Levis on the St. Lawrence River in Quebec. The harsh nature of Maine's weather reared its ugly head during this trip in the form of a strong windstorm on October 12 and 13 and a drenching rain from the 19th to the 21st. Arnold and his men also encountered three early season snowstorms, the largest of these was a six-inch snow on the 24th and 25th of October, with smaller snowstorms on the 3rd–4th and 7th of November. Maine's weather certainly added to the hardships of the expedition and Arnold's force of men was greatly reduced by the time they reached Quebec.

There is no doubt that Mainers have always had to deal with very dynamic and potentially life-altering weather, but at the same time, the beauty and natural wonders of Maine are also directly related to the state's weather and climate. Our modern landscape actually began to develop under the climatic conditions of 10,000 years ago, a short step back in time from a geological perspective (Fig. 1.1). At that time, the entire state was covered by the last great ice sheet that spread over large portions of North America. The erosion associated with the moving ice carved out great portions of the landscape in Maine. Sediments deposited directly from the ice or from melt water flowing from the glaciers produced many of the landforms that make up great expanses of the state's landscape. With warmer conditions at the end of the last glaciation, melting ice helped to raise sea level, thereby producing the rugged coastline of Maine (Fig. 1.2).

Our present-day weather conditions now highlight this wondrous landscape. Dif-

Figure 1.1. Examples of glaciated features in the landscape of Maine. On the left is a photograph of the Beehive, Acadia National Park. This feature is a roche moutonnée formed by glacial erosion and indicative of the direction of ice flow. Ice flowed from the right (north) of the hill (long gentle slope) to the left (south) of the hill (short steep slope). Photograph from Greg Zielinski. On the right is a photograph of Balancing Rock, Acadia National Park. This large boulder was placed on top of the Bubbles by the last ice sheet. Photograph from Chris Zielinski.

Figure 1.2 (facing page). Example of the rocky coastline of Maine showing Bass Harbor Light, Mount Desert Island. Photograph by Chris Zielinski.

ferent cloud types form under different weather conditions leading to great variability in a single vista from one day to the next. Coastal areas are frequently shrouded in fog, a nemesis for some, but the source of interesting lighting for photographers. A gorgeous rainbow against the dark sky of a summer shower or thunderstorm enhances the state's scenery. Furthermore, how can one talk about the beauty of the state without mentioning the glorious colors of autumn. Our weather and climate is greatly responsible for many of the most delightful parts of Maine's culture and the interactions between Maine's people and environment.

The dynamic nature of Maine's weather can cause it to change very quickly over a short period of time or even as you simply drive down the road. On the other hand, great differences in weather conditions can be encountered from year to year, such as going from a very frigid, snowy winter one year to a warm winter with limited snowfall the next. This book will help you understand what controls the great variability in Maine's weather and why it differs so much across the state. At the same time, you will be able to evaluate how Maine's weather and climate have changed over time and think about what continuing changes may mean for our future. Rest assured, our climate has always been changing and it will continue to do so.

2

THE "QUICKIE" GUIDE TO WEATHER

Sometimes the weather-related terms used by local forecasters or individuals in various parts of the media are unknown or many people may be unclear as to what they actually mean. It may be frustrating when you are listening for "just the forecast," but these other terms are added to the description of weather conditions. Have no fear, for I'll explain many of those terms. You may still want the "weather person" to get to the forecast, but at least now you'll understand what these individuals are talking about.

In addition to the words and phrases commonly used by forecasters, it may also be unclear just what the difference is between weather and climate. Weather is the condition of the atmosphere at any given moment at any given place. Climate, on the other hand, is average weather over a long period of time or over an area larger than a single location. Examples of climate include the average temperature for the month of January in Portland, the average daily high on September 18 for Presque Isle, and the average annual precipitation for the state of Maine. Both weather and climate are part of meteorology, which is the study of the atmosphere, although the study of climate itself is climatology. Meteorologists study the atmosphere and that includes many different components such as weather forecasting, probably the part of the profession most familiar to the general public.

The definition of the seasons may not mean the same thing from one person to another. After all, one has only to remember the last one-foot snowstorm that hit several weeks after the first day of spring. The common use of the terms winter, spring, summer ,and fall comes from the position of the sun relative to the equator and the Tropic of Cancer (Northern Hemisphere) and Tropic of Capricorn (Southern Hemisphere). The seasons are solar based and so are not completely connected to local weather conditions. It is true that the first day of winter is on or about December 21 in Maine, and in the Northern Hemisphere as a whole. It is the day with the least amount of daylight during the year and it is around the coldest time of the year. However, because of various factors (see chapter 5), the average coldest day of the year in Maine actually falls in mid- to late January or early February. So we can also classify the seasons by the coldest 90 days of the year (climatological winter) and by the warmest 90 days of the year (climatological summer). The average hottest day of the year occurs almost one month after the day with the longest amount of daylight—about June 21 or the first day of summer. Climatological spring and fall would then be the 90 days that fall between the coldest and warmest days of climatological winter and summer.

Of course, all Mainers know the "real" seasons are defined by neither of these factors, but rather by the impact on one's lifestyle. True spring is in reality more appropriately named "mud season" and the first part of true summer is "blackfly season." These two are perhaps the most well known of the "real" seasons of Maine, but others can readily be described as beach season (summer), skiing or snowmobiling season (winter), and leaf season (fall), to name a few possibilities. The timing of these "real" seasons, as well as the timing of the climatological seasons, differs across the state, another reason why understanding our weather and climate is not a simple task.

WHAT THE FORECASTERS TELL YOU

A typical listing of current conditions, whether from local television or radio, may include terms such as temperature, barometric pressure, wind speed and direction, including gusts, and relative humidity. In some cases, more detailed accounts of current conditions may be provided by including additional terms in the summary, such as dew point or the existing wind chill or heat index. Specific aspects of each of these components of weather will be presented in later chapters.

■ TEMPERATURE

Nearly everyone is familiar with the term temperature, but what does it actually represent? Technically, the temperature that we record is a measure of the average speed of air molecules, with greater speeds meaning higher temperatures and lower speeds producing lower temperatures. A more simple definition, however, is the quantity measured by a thermometer—certainly a definition we can all relate to. Temperature is measured in three different units. The scale used in the United States is Fahrenheit (°F), while most of the rest of the world uses the Celsius scale (°C). The exact conversion between the two scales is °F = 1.8C° + 32, with the two scales being equal at –40°. Absolute temperature is measured in Kelvin (°K), but because of the large numbers and ranges involved, that unit is not used to report air temperatures.

Degree Days: Heating and cooling degree-days were developed during the energy crisis of the mid-1970s as guidelines for determining yearly energy needs. They are based on the average daily temperature relative to 65°F. The thought is that average daily temperatures below 65°F require heating of the household or building, hence the term heating degree-day. Average daily temperatures above 65°F require energy to cool the household or building, thus the term cooling degree-day.

■ HUMIDITY

One of the most important characteristics of our planet that allows the existence of life is the presence of water in all three of its phases, solid (ice), liquid, and gas (water vapor). The amount of the water in the atmosphere at any one location is an important characteristic that has many ramifications for the weather. The most common form water takes in the atmosphere is the gaseous phase, thus the amount of water vapor present in the air is an important forecast tool. The term humidity is a reflection of how much water vapor is in the air.

Relative Humidity: The most common number presented by forecasters to describe the moisture content of the atmosphere. It is actually the ratio of the vapor pressure (the pressure exerted by the water-vapor molecules) to the saturation vapor pressure (when the pressure of the water-vapor molecules is equal to that of a surface in either the liquid or ice phase of water). The relative humidity of the air can be measured and expressed as a percentage, with 100% relative humidity meaning the air is completely saturated with water vapor.

Dew Point: The temperature at which water vapor condenses to form liquid water. It, too, is indicative of the moisture content of the air.

Clouds: The visible form in the sky of the many tiny water droplets that accumulate when water vapor condenses in rising air. The type of cloud is determined by its form and many times a forecaster will mention the type of clouds one could expect to see during the day. The very high wispy clouds are cirrus and they often are the first type of cloud observed as a storm system approaches. Very puffy clouds that show some vertical growth are cumulus clouds and when the vertical growth is limited, these are characteristic of fair weather. However, when they grow vertically to great heights they often form thunderheads or cumulonimbus clouds. Stratus clouds are layered clouds and they are the most common type of cloud associated with precipitation. There are many combinations of these different cloud types.

Fog: When enough water vapor condenses very close to the earth's surface it forms a cloud that may be only a few feet above the ground. This is fog.

Heat Index: How often do you hear the phrase, "it is not the heat, but the humidity"? This phrase reflects how the moisture content of the air increases the impact of air temperature on humans and other animals during the summer or warm-season months. The body cools itself by the evaporation of sweat, but when the humidity is high, the perspiration we generate is not able to evaporate, thereby reducing the body's ability to cool off. To make sure that this potentially dangerous situation is known to the general public, the heat index is often reported along with air temperature during those "sticky" days of summer. The heat index indicates what the air temperature actually feels like (that is, the apparent temperature) to the body given the humidity conditions that exist (Table 2.1). A high heat index can lead to dehydration and heat stroke at a much quicker rate than would occur with the same temperature and lower humidity levels.

■ ATMOSPHERIC PRESSURE

Air is drawn toward the center of the earth by gravity, so pressure is created at the earth's surface by the weight of our atmosphere. Forecasters are more likely to use the term barometric pressure when reporting atmospheric conditions, because it is measured with a barometer. The unit of atmospheric pressure used in the United States is inches of mercury (in. Hg), because mercury is the fluid in the standard barometer. The more common unit of pressure around the world and the unit often used to describe the strength of storm systems is the millibar (mb).

Surface: Atmospheric pressure decreases with elevation because there is less of the earth's atmosphere above someone at a given altitude versus somebody at sea level. It is for this reason that when you hear the pressure given for a particular location, that pressure is converted to what it would be if the location was at sea level. This allows comparisons to be made from one site to another without worrying about differences in pressure caused by differences in elevation. The average pressure at the earth's surface is 29.91 in. Hg or 1013 mb. Weather maps shown on television and on the Web frequently show lines of equal surface pressure, referred to as isobars.

Upper-air Pressure: As you move higher and higher away from the surface of the Earth there is less atmosphere above you. The result is that the pressure decreases as you go upward. In fact, it decreases very quickly with height—the reason you feel light-headed and feel pressure on your eardrums at higher altitudes. This is why the cabin of a passenger jet is pressurized. In addition, the pressure at different levels of the atmosphere is critical to our weather here at the earth's surface. That is the reason forecasters will often mention upper air patterns or characteristics when talking about how strong an approaching storm will be, particularly in the case of nor'easters. Upper air patterns are a reflection of the air pressure patterns at different levels of the earth's atmosphere. These patterns are important because they will often dictate the direction and speed of weather systems at the surface. Upper-air pressure patterns can also directly impact the weather at the surface even when there is no obvious weather feature at the surface.

Table 2.1. Heat Index.

Air Temperature (°F)

% Relative Humidity	80	82	84	86	88	90	92	94	96	98	100	102	104	106	108	110
40	80	81	83	85	88	91	94	97	101	105	109	114	119	124	130	136
45	80	82	84	87	89	93	96	100	104	109	114	119	124	130	137	
50	81	83	85	88	91	95	99	102	108	113	118	124	131	137		
55	81	84	86	89	93	97	101	106	112	117	124	130	137			
60	82	84	88	91	95	100	105	110	116	123	129	137				
65	82	85	89	93	98	103	108	114	121	128	136					
70	83	86	90	95	100	106	112	119	126	134						
75	84	88	92	97	103	109	116	124	132							
80	84	89	94	100	106	110	121	129								
85	85	90	96	102	110	117	126	136								
90	86	91	98	105	113	122	131									
95	86	93	100	108	117	127										
100	87	95	103	112	121	132										

Note: Heat index in light gray also referred to as apparent temperature. A Category I heat index (apparent temperature >130°F, in **black**) means heatstroke or sunstroke is highly likely. Category II heat index (apparent temperature 105—129°F, in **dark gray**) means sunstroke, muscle cramps, or heat exhaustion likely. Category III heat index (apparent temperature 90-104°F, light gray) means sunstroke, muscle cramps and heat exhaustion possible. Category IV heat index (apparent temperature 80—90°F) means fatigue possible. Prolonged exposure and physical activity greatly increases the likelihood of the impacts within each category of heat index. From the National Weather Service, National Oceanic and Atmospheric Administration.

High-pressure System: One of the major circulation features found at the earth's surface, high-pressure systems, or highs, form when air is descending from upper levels of the atmosphere. They are also referred to as anticyclones. This descending air increases atmospheric pressure at the surface and results in an area of pressure higher than that of the surrounding region. A high is usually associated with nice weather because descending air prevents abundant air from rising from the earth's surface. Rising air will cool, condense, and form clouds that may eventually become large enough to produce precipitation. Airflow around a high-pressure system is clockwise in the Northern Hemisphere because of the Coriolis Effect (a force caused by the rotation of the earth). Together with the descending air, the result is that air will move outward from the center of the high-pressure system in this clockwise pattern. The center of the high-pressure system on a weather map is designated by a blue H. Highs often dominate a large part of the country.

Low-pressure System: The other major circulation feature at the surface is the low-pressure system, or low. These are also referred to as cyclones. Lows are characterized by rising air, resulting in an area of lower pressure at the surface compared to that of the surrounding region. The process of rising air is referred to as convection. Rising air cools and water vapor condenses to form water droplets and clouds. Precipitation may eventually fall from these clouds. As a result, storms are areas of low-pressure. The air moves in a counter-clockwise motion around a low in the Northern Hemisphere. As air moves upward in the center of a low, more air moves in toward the low's center to replace the rising air. The result is that motion around a low-pressure system is toward the center in a counter-clockwise direction. The center of the low-pressure system on a weather map is designated by a red L. Unlike high-pressure systems, lows are, overall, smaller pressure systems.

■ WIND

Wind is the movement of air relative to the earth's surface. There are several factors that dictate the direction and speed of wind, but the primary cause, as so often discussed by forecasters, is the difference in pressure between high- and low-pressure systems. This difference in pressure over the distance between the two systems is the pressure gradient. The higher the gradient, as shown on a weather map by closely spaced isobars, the faster the wind will blow. The lower the gradient, that is, widely spaced isobars, the slower the wind will blow. Essentially there is minimal wind or calm conditions immediately under the center of a high-pressure system. The horizontal movement of airflow is referred to as advection.

Wind Direction: Potentially one of the more confusing items presented by a forecaster is the wind direction. Wind direction always indicates the direction from which the wind is blowing. For instance, a north wind means that the wind is blowing from the north toward the south.

Wind Speed: There are two methods to evaluate wind speed. One way is via sustained wind speed. The second is the wind gust, a brief increase in wind speed. The highest recorded wind averaged over a two-minute period is often used to determine the maximum wind speed for a day. Wind speeds in the United States are recorded either in miles per hour (mph) or in knots. Knots are nautical miles, which are equal to 1.15 standard miles—meaning a wind speed of 100 knots is equal to 115 mph. Other places in the world present wind speeds in meters/second (m/s) or sometimes in kilometers per hour (kph).

Wind Chill: During the winter or cold-season months, the term wind chill is almost always reported along with air temperature, particularly on those cold mornings when strong winds drive the cold to your bones. The wind chill index is used to quantify heat loss from the body under cold conditions, because wind blowing across bare skin makes that loss more. The wind chill index was recalculated in 2001 (Table 2.2) and it is some-

Table 2.2 Wind Chill.

Air Temperature (°F)

		40	35	30	25	20	15	10	5	0	-5	-10	-15	-20	-25	-30	-35	-40	-45
Wind Speed (mph)	**5**	36	31	25	19	13	7	1	-5	-11	-16	-22	-28	-34	-40	-46	-52	-57	-63
	10	34	27	21	15	9	3	-4	-10	-16	-22	-28	-35	-41	-47	-53	-59	-66	-72
	15	32	25	19	13	6	0	-7	-13	-19	-26	-32	-39	-45	-51	-58	-64	-71	-77
	20	30	24	17	11	4	-2	-9	-15	-22	-29	-35	-42	-48	-55	-61	-68	-74	-81
	25	29	23	16	9	3	-4	-11	-17	-24	-31	-37	-44	-51	-58	-64	-71	-78	-84
	30	28	22	15	8	1	-5	-12	-19	-26	-33	-39	-46	-53	-60	-67	-73	-80	-87
	35	28	21	14	7	0	-7	-14	-21	-27	-34	-41	-48	-55	-62	-69	-76	-82	-89
	40	27	20	13	6	-1	-8	-15	-22	-29	-36	-43	-50	-57	-64	-71	-78	-84	-91
	45	26	19	12	5	-2	-9	-16	-23	-30	-37	-44	-51	-58	-65	-72	-79	-86	-93
	50	26	19	12	4	-3	-10	-17	-24	-31	-38	-45	-52	-60	-67	-74	-81	-88	-95
	55	25	18	11	4	-3	-11	-18	-25	-32	-39	-46	-54	-61	-68	-75	-82	-89	-97
	60	25	17	10	3	-4	-11	-19	-26	-33	-40	-48	-55	-62	-69	-76	-84	-91	-98

Note: Wind chill values calculated by wind chill (°F) = $35.74 + 0.6125T - 35.75(V^{0.16})$ + $0.4275T(V^{0.16})$, where T = air temperature (°F) and V = wind velocity (mph). Frostbite may occur in 30 minutes as indicated by numbers **black**, in 10 minutes by numbers in **dark gray**, and in 5 minutes by numbers in light gray. From the National Weather Service, National Oceanic and Atmospheric Administration.

times described as the equivalent temperature exposed skin would feel if there was no wind. No matter how you define wind chill, it can be very dangerous, leading to quick onset of hypothermia and frostbite.

■ PRECIPITATION

Precipitation is the other weather phenomenon that most people pay attention to. By definition, precipitation is any liquid or solid water originating in the atmosphere that ends up hitting the ground. This is in contrast to virga, which is falling liquid or solid water that evaporates prior to reaching the earth's surface. Virga is often observed as vertical wisps or streaks below clouds.

Rain: When liquid precipitation falls in drops greater than 0.5 mm in diameter, it is classified as rain. Droplets that are less than 0.5 mm in diameter are classified as drizzle. Perhaps the only way that most individuals can tell the difference, considering what it might take to measure an individual drop, is that visibility becomes much more reduced in drizzle than in light rain. A rain shower is defined as a brief period when rainfall intensity changes frequently—sometimes quite rapidly.

Snow: Snow is frozen precipitation that is composed of white or translucent ice crystals that often take a branched form. Accumulations of these ice crystals produce snowflakes. Snow showers are the same as rain showers in that they are brief periods of changing snowfall intensity. When the snow shower only lasts for a short period of time then it is considered to be snow flurries. The other common term associated with snow is blizzard. Blizzard conditions exist when there are high winds that produce reduced visibility from falling or blowing snow. The National Weather Service defines blizzard conditions as winds of 30 knots (35 mph) or greater with sufficient snow in the air to reduce visibility to less than a quarter mile. At one time, the definition of a blizzard also included the presence of temperatures of 20°F or lower, but that aspect is no longer included in the definition of a blizzard. It is noteworthy that blizzard conditions can exist without falling snow since the definition of a blizzard is based on wind and visibility. This situation can occur when recently fallen powdery snow is whipped-up by strong winds, thus creating treacherous driving conditions. Sometimes the term ground blizzard is used to describe this situation. Whiteout conditions can occur with either windblown or very rapidly falling snow and it is dangerous because visibility becomes seriously impaired as the ground and sky become impossible to differentiate.

Sleet: Essentially sleet can also be defined as ice pellets—solid precipitation consisting of transparent or translucent pellets of ice that are 5 mm or less in diameter. The pellets may come in various shapes, with one defining characteristic being the sound they make when they hit the ground. They also bounce when they hit a hard surface. These characteristics are much different than those of freezing rain.

Freezing Rain: Unlike sleet, which is already ice when it hits the ground, freezing rain is liquid precipitation that freezes upon impact with an object. Freezing rain produces a glaze on the ground, including roadways, sidewalks, and other exposed objects.

Hail: Almost always a warm-weather phenomenon, unlike sleet and freezing rain, hail is precipitation in the form of balls or irregular lumps of ice. Concentric rings often make-up individual hailstones, which can range from pea- to grapefruit-sized. They form in very intense convective situations, such as severe thunderstorms.

■ FRONTS

A front is the zone that marks the boundary between two air masses of very different densities. The representation of this zone on a weather map is a line indicating the type of front. Specific types of air or air mass characteristics are often markedly different on each side of the front, as is wind direction. The contrasting winds result in converging currents that produce rising air and, very often, precipitation. This is the reason frontal zones are frequently accompanied by areas of precipitation.

Air Mass: A widespread body of air with similar characteristics throughout the entire area covered by this body of air. The two main characteristics that identify an air mass and the resulting density are the temperature and moisture conditions, or humidity. The air mass will take on the characteristics of the earth's surface over which it develops. The major types of air masses are combinations of temperature conditions, such as tropical (warm to hot) and polar (cool to cold), and moisture conditions, such as maritime (humid) and continental (dry). The greatest contrast in air masses will occur when a humid and hot air mass (maritime tropical) meets a dry and cold air mass (continental polar).

Cold Front: A cold front occurs when a denser air mass is moving into a warmer, less dense air mass. The front marks the zone where this cold air is pushing under the warmer air, resulting in rising air and usually a narrow zone of showers or, depending on the season, possibly thunderstorms, some of which may be quite strong. Winds usually come out of the northwest following the passage of the front. The cold front is colored blue on a typical weather map, with triangles pointing in the direction of movement.

Warm Front: A warm front marks the zone where a warmer, less dense air mass is overriding a cooler, more dense air mass in front of it. The overriding produces rising air and precipitation. Unlike the passage of a cold front, a warm front is more often characterized by a broad area of precipitation, though it is often less intense precipitation than that associated with a cold front. The warm front is colored red on a weather map, with semi-circles facing in the direction of movement.

Stationary Front: There may be times when two contrasting air masses meet, but neither is strong enough to push the other out of the way. This may be because the contrast between the two is not great enough for one of the air masses to push under or override the other, or the upper-air winds may not be strong enough to push the weather systems along. The front resulting from these scenarios is a stationary front. The front marks the location where these contrasting air masses come together. The stationary front is often marked by converging air, causing the air to rise, condense, and form precipitation. Low-pressure systems will often move along a stationary front, thereby increasing precipitation in areas over which the low-pressure system moves. The symbol on a weather map for a stationary front is alternating cold (triangles) and warm (semi-circles) front symbols on opposite sides of the front.

Occluded Front: Occasionally a weather map will show a purplish-colored front extending from a low-pressure system and ending at the junction of a cold and warm front. This situation is especially possible in the case of some nor'easters as they approach or move through Maine. This is called an occluded front and it marks the contrast between cool and cold air with warmer air trapped above the surface front. Occluded fronts commonly develop when a storm, like a nor'easter, reaches maximum intensity. As a result, the occluded front is frequently associated with an area of abundant precipitation. The symbol for an occluded front on a weather map is alternating cold and warm front symbols on the same side of the front (as opposed to the alternating sides for a stationary front) pointing in the direction in which the front is moving.

■ WATCHES AND WARNINGS

One of the most important roles played by the National Weather Service and subsequently by local forecasters is informing the general public about the possibility that a particular weather event may bring harm to people or produce damage to personal property. The National Weather Service issues specific advisories, watches, and warnings as a means to alert people about weather conditions that could produce such a situation. In general, watches are issued when conditions may lead to the formation of the weather event of concern, whereas a warning is issued when the particular weather phenomenon is imminent or has been spotted. Here are brief explanations of some of the hazardous weather notices issued by the National Weather Service.

Wind Chill Advisory: This advisory is issued when wind chills may be life threatening if appropriate action is not taken. Conditions needed to issue the advisory vary, but they will often be issued when wind chills are expected to reach below -20°F and almost always when they are expected to reach the −30° to −35°F range or below.

Heat Advisory or Warning: A heat advisory is issued 12 hours prior to the time when the heat index is expected to reach 105°F for 3 or more hours during the day or nighttime lows are expected to remain above 80°F. The advisory is upgraded to a warning when the heat index reaches 115°F. Heat advisories are not very common in Maine, and a heat warning would be rare, indeed.

Severe Thunderstorm Watch: Conditions are appropriate for the formation of a severe thunderstorm. A severe thunderstorm has winds that exceed 58 mph with the possibility of 3/4-inch diameter or greater hail. Watches often are issued for a period of 4–8 hours for broad areas of a region.

Severe Thunderstorm Warning: A severe thunderstorm has been sighted or indicated on radar. The warning will be issued for the area that the thunderstorm or storms are moving toward, and the warning will often include the time period when the severe thunderstorm is expected to move into a particular county or city.

Tornado Watch: Conditions are appropriate for the formation of a tornado, usually over a wide area.

Tornado Warning: A tornado warning means that either an official weather spotter, such as a member of the police force, has seen a tornado on the ground or has seen a funnel cloud, or when radar indicates that there is rotation in a severe thunderstorm. They are usually issued for a period of 30 minutes.

Winter Weather Advisory: Minor accumulation of winter precipitation, including any combination of snow, sleet, or freezing rain, is possible after the next 24-hour period. Potential snow accumulations are not expected to be great enough to meet the criteria for a warning.

Winter Storm Watch: Significant accumulation of winter precipitation, including any combination of snow, sleet or freezing rain, is possible over the next 24- to 36-hour period. Potential snow accumulations for a watch are usually greater than 6 inches, but it varies by location.

Winter Storm Warning: Significant accumulation of winter precipitation, including any combination of snow, sleet or freezing rain, is probable within the next 24-hour period. Potential snow accumulations for warnings are usually greater than 6 inches, but it varies by location.

High Wind Advisory: Issued when high winds may be a hazard. Criteria vary from state to state, but they often are issued when sustained winds of 25 to 39 mph or gusts up to 57 mph are expected.

High Wind Warning: Issued when high winds may be a hazard. Criteria vary from state to state, but they often are issued when sustained winds of at least 40 mph or gusts exceeding 57 mph are expected.

Tropical Storm Watch and Warning: Issued when tropical force winds (39–74 mph) originating from a tropical storm that is passing by a region or may make landfall sometime in the next 24–36-hours. The watch is upgraded to a warning when these conditions are expected within the next 24 hours.

Hurricane Watch and Warning: Issued when hurricane force winds (> 74 mph) originating from a hurricane that is passing by a region or may make landfall sometime in the next 24–36-hours. The watch is upgraded to a warning when these conditions are expected within the next 24 hours.

In addition to these warnings, the National Weather Service will issue specific warnings applicable to mariners and, in the case of Maine, conditions on the Gulf of Maine. These warnings are primarily based on high wind speeds that cause increasingly dangerous wave heights as the severity of the warning increases. These advisories or warnings are commonly associated with conditions from mid-latitude circulation systems—like a nor'easter—as opposed to those from a tropical system—like a tropical storm or hurricane. In the latter case, tropical storm or hurricane watches and warnings would be issued.

Small Craft Advisory: Sustained winds or frequent gusts ranging between 25 and 33 knots and/or seas or waves 5 to 7 feet and greater, area dependent.

Gale Warning: A warning of sustained surface winds, or frequent gusts, ranging from 34–47 knots (39–54 mph), either predicted or occurring, and not directly associated with a tropical cyclone.

Storm Warning: A warning of sustained surface winds, or frequent gusts, ranging from 48–63 knots (55–73 mph), either predicted or occurring, and not directly associated with a tropical cyclone.

3

THE BIG PICTURE

Maine's variable weather and climate is the direct result of several different factors. There are permanent, ongoing factors related to global and regional aspects of the entire climate system, as well as to other parts of Maine's environment, such as its landscape and the ocean. In addition, there are other factors that have periodic effects on the state's weather. Here are some brief descriptions of the forces that influence and ultimately control Maine's weather.

■ PERMANENT FACTORS

The following factors are considered to be permanent or fairly consistent over a few centuries to a millennium. There are some variations within these factors, but for the most part, they are fairly consistent within a range of limits as to how they influence the weather.

Maine's Location

Maine extends from 43°05'N latitude in Kittery to just north of 47°25'N latitude (St. Francis River, T20, R11 and 12) with the 45°N latitude extending across the state just north of such towns as Rangeley, Old Town, and Pembroke and through the center of Hudson. This puts Maine exactly halfway between the North Pole and the equator. As a result, the state is in the middle of the battleground between the cold, dry air found in the sub-polar and polar regions and the hot, humid air from the sub-tropics and tropics. Areas of contrasting air masses produce many aspects of the weather in mid-latitudes, and particularly, certain types of storms.

Maine's Landscape

The landscape of Maine is just one of the reasons it is so enjoyable to live here and why so many tourists come here. At the same time, it plays a great role in the kind of weather we have. The state can be divided into three general landscape zones. The first zone is the hills and mountains of western and northwestern Maine. Coastal areas represent the second zone; and the third zone is essentially made up of the foothills and open areas through the center and into the far north of the state. The hills affect weather and climate as their elevation leads to cooler conditions that can result in snow instead of the rain that may occur closer to the coast, and the hills may have a great impact on precipitation amounts as well. The windward side of the mountains may help produce greater amounts of from a storm, while the lee side of the mountains may be shadowed from the storm, resulting in lower amounts of precipitation.

Ocean Currents and the Gulf of Maine

Because of water's great heat capacity compared to the land, the ocean is a great modifier of weather and climate. Water has a much greater ability to maintain its temperature, but land temperature can change very rapidly. For example, the ocean does not heat up as much as the land during the summer, and it maintains its heat during the winter, while the land loses its heat to a much greater extent. As a result, immediate coastal areas are cooler during the summer and warmer during the winter compared to inland areas.

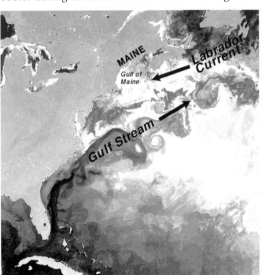

Figure 3.1. Satellite image showing the cold Labrador Current flowing into the Gulf of Maine and the warm Gulf Stream moving off the coast. Image from NOAA, Southeast US Atlantic Coastal Ocean Observing System (SEACOOS), www.seacoos.org.

The influence of the Gulf of Maine on the state's weather is enhanced by the fact that it is a cool water body compared to the waters of southern New England. The surface waters that move into the Gulf of Maine come from the Labrador Current (Fig. 3.1). Because this is a cold water current, the waters in the gulf do not warm up very much, even during the summer, especially compared to the warmer waters of the Gulf Stream, the current that influences the weather of Connecticut, Rhode Island, Cape Cod, and the islands of Massachusetts. Yet surface waters in the Gulf of Maine remain much warmer than the land during the winter, despite the presence of the Labrador Current.

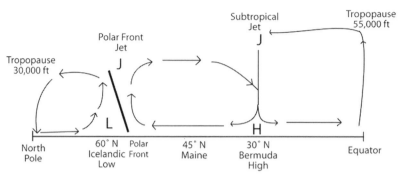

Figure 3.2. Schematic diagram showing the vertical component of general air flow from the tropics to the poles with position of the jet streams and major circulation systems in the Atlantic Ocean.

Global Circulation Patterns

The nature of airflow and the circulation patterns in the Northern Hemisphere are functions of how heat is distributed throughout the planet. The equator receives a greater amount of solar radiation than other areas, so there is a net movement of heat and energy from the equator toward the poles. When you add the rotation of the earth, the result is a very distinct nature of air movement northward toward the pole. The greater heating at the equator causes an overall rising of the air and a series of low-pressure systems around the tropics (Fig. 3.2). This air rises and moves toward the poles, cooling and becoming denser. Consequently, it begins to sink back toward the earth's surface, producing semi-permanent high-pressure systems in the subtropical regions of the oceans. The subtropical high in the North Atlantic Ocean is the Bermuda-Azores High, or Bermuda High for short (Fig. 3.3). Highs such as this, along with other circulation systems, are described as semi-permanent because they are almost always there, but the center of the circulation system may move and the intensity of the system varies.

The sinking air associated with the Bermuda High spreads laterally, rotating in the clockwise pattern of the Northern Hemisphere. The air moving northward eventually runs into the dense cold air moving southward from the polar region. The front that forms where these air masses collide is the polar front. In addition, the cold dense air from the polar regions forces the air moving northward to rise, producing a series of semi-permanent sub-polar lows in the more northern regions of the oceans. In the North Atlantic, the semi-permanent low-pressure system is called the Icelandic Low (Fig. 3.3). The air rising in the region of these sub-polar lows spreads northward toward the pole, where the air then sinks, completing the cycle. Rising air in the sub-polar lows will also spread south again, sinking in the area of the sub-tropical high. This series of cycles in air movement plays a major role in the overall distribution of energy and the development of weather systems and climatic conditions.

Along with this vertical movement of air around the planet, the rotation of the earth also produces a horizontal pattern of air movement. The easiest way to remember these patterns is to think about the airflow around the semi-permanent pressure

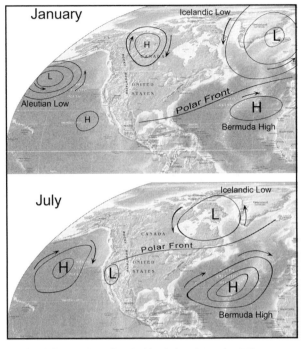

Figure 3.3. Location of major North American circulation systems and average position of the polar front in January (top) and July (bottom).

systems that form via vertical air motion. The counterclockwise flow around the low-pressure systems in the tropics, together with the clockwise flow around the Bermuda High produces the Inter-Tropical Convergence Zone (ITCZ) at the equator. These are the trade winds and those in the Northern Hemisphere are called the northeast trades. The other extreme is in the polar region, where the permanent high-pressure systems and the counter-clockwise flow around the sub-polar lows (like the Icelandic Low) produce the polar easterlies in the Northern Hemisphere. Between the polar and equatorial extremes lie the mid-latitudes, which include Maine. This part of the planet lies between the counter-clockwise flow around the sub-polar lows and the clockwise flow around the sub-tropical highs. The result is the westerlies, the flow from west to east over the mid-latitudes that drives all the weather systems that influence Maine. The westerlies not only exist at the surface, but they also exist in the upper levels of our atmosphere. In the case of Maine, the two dominant systems that produce the westerlies and highly influence much of our weather are the Icelandic Low and the Bermuda High.

Within the westerlies is an area of particularly fast moving air that drives all the weather systems at the surface. This region of fast moving air is the jet stream, and it is essentially the primary steering current for the weather systems and location of various air masses in the mid-latitudes. The surface representation of the jet stream is the polar front; thus the jet stream generally separates cold, dry polar air from warm, humid tropical air. The jet stream's effect on our weather is a function of the pattern it takes. One pattern is referred to as zonal flow, where the jet stream pattern is primarily west to east with very little or no north to south component (Fig. 3.4). This pattern produces overall mild conditions across Maine depending on which side of the jet stream the state is located. The other extreme is meridional flow, where there are major north-south shifts, or bends, in the jet stream.

This sinuous pattern allows polar air to move toward the equator, while at the same time, tropical air is able to move farther north. The region where the polar air moves south is referred to as a trough in the westerlies, while the tropical air moves north under a ridge in the westerlies. The resulting contrast in air masses is what produces so much of our day-to-day weather, especially the major storm systems that move across the country. The exact location of the troughs and ridges dictates the type of air mass that will dominate Maine's weather. Their location also determines the path that storms will take, particularly important in determining whether Maine will be on the warm rainy eastern side of a winter storm or the cold snowy western side of the storm. It will also help determine where the zone of "slop" occurs, that is the region of mixed precipitation that can vary from snow to sleet to freezing rain to rain.

Occasionally, a situation occurs in the upper atmosphere when a low-pressure system forms outside the jet stream. When this happens, the low is not pushed along by the strong winds of the jet stream, but moves very slowly eastward across the country. This is referred to as a cut-off low and it may end up producing precipitation that remains over an area for several days. This scenario can often cause flooding—cut-off lows have produced record rainfalls in Maine. In fact, one of the top ten major weather events in Maine over the last 200 years was the direct result of a cut-off low. (See Chapter 13).

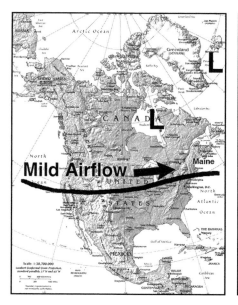

Figure 3.4. Example of a zonal pattern of the jet stream across the United States (left) and a meridional pattern of the jet stream (right). The zonal pattern is very characteristic of the positive or warm mode of the North Atlantic Oscillation (NAO), whereas the meridional pattern shown is very characteristic of the negative or cold mode of the NAO. See text for discussion.

■ NON-PERMANENT FACTORS

In addition to the consistent factors controlling Maine's weather, there are factors that may influence conditions one year but not the next, or that may exert an influence over several years then not be a factor over the next ten or more years. The following factors may be quite variable as to when they influence Maine's weather and the level or intensity of that influence.

High-pressure Systems

Although low-pressure systems (storms) probably get most of the attention, the real control on the day-to-day movement of circulation systems across the country is the high-pressure systems. They are much bigger systems than lows and because they are colder than lows, air masses associated with them are very dense. As a result, they are harder to move, and will push other systems in front of them. The high-pressure systems that form and move across North America usually start their journey in northern Canada where cold dry air is so common (Fig. 3.5). These highs move across the United States and are responsible for the cool to cold air that moves into Maine. As they move away from the area, they may pull in the flow off the ocean that is both cool and humid. The highs that move more toward southern Maine bring the warmer, humid air into the region. Sometimes the high-pressure systems that affect the state are strong enough to remain in their position for a long period of time. This is a blocking high. This scenario leads to either long cold and/or dry spells or long hot, humid periods. Either way, highs ultimately exert a tremendous influence on our day-to-day weather.

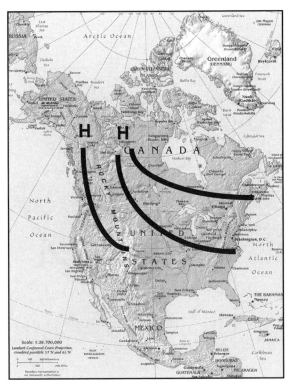

Figure 3.5. General paths that high-pressure systems take when moving across North America.

Storm Tracks

There are several major tracks that storms frequently follow as they migrate across the United States (Fig. 3.6). These tracks indicate the general zones or paths that storms are known to take. Some tracks are more active at certain times of the year than at others, with the biggest difference in activity occurring between summer and winter. Given the variety of paths storms may take and the variability in the numbers of storms that follow specific paths, storm tracks are considered to be a non-permanent control on Maine's weather.

Individual tracks are named for the location where the storm forms, and there are several primary sources for storms moving across the country. The process of storm development is technically referred to as

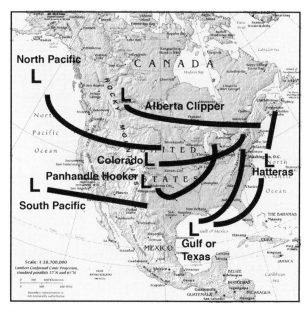

Figure 3.6. Common storm tracks across the United States.

cyclogenesis. One source is in the Pacific Ocean, particularly in the Gulf of Alaska. This is one of the most active areas in the world for storm development, primarily during the cold season. The Aleutian Low (Fig. 3.3) is the most common source of many of the storms that move across the United States. The other most common area of storm development is just to the east of the Rocky Mountains, that is, on the lee side (the side sheltered from the prevailing winds) of the mountains. Actually, many of these storms originate in the Pacific Ocean, but as they travel across the Rocky Mountains, they are compressed, spreading out and losing their form as a distinct low-pressure system. Once they move away from the mountains, they are able to reform to the point that a distinct low-pressure center is identifiable. This process is referred to as lee-side cyclogenesis, reflecting the formation of storms on the lee side of the mountains. A third area of cyclogenesis exists in the Gulf of Mexico and along the eastern coast of the United States. Mainers are well aware of storm development along the Atlantic coast, as these systems have a major impact on the state.

Perhaps the most interesting aspect of the storm tracks that affect Maine is that nearly every major track across the United States has the potential to move across the state or at least to be close enough to affect the state's weather. This is true for New England as a whole. The reason for this is that as storms move across the U. S. they are often guided toward the Icelandic Low in the North Atlantic with help from the flow around the north and west side of the Bermuda High. Although almost any track can influence Maine's weather, there are several that are most influential and well worth watching. This is especially true during the cold season as storm development is much more prevalent. The greater contrast between air masses of polar and mid-latitude regions and those of the tropics is the driving force for a greater frequency of storms during the winter and transition (spring and fall) seasons than in the summer.

The most common tracks storms follow to Maine are the Alberta Clipper and the combination of the Atlantic (Hatteras) and Gulf of Mexico tracks. The Alberta Clipper gets its name not only because it forms around southern Alberta, Canada, but also because they tend to be fast moving systems. Consequently, they are often not big precipitation producers. Sometimes, however, they may move into the Gulf of Maine and intensify greatly, producing a large coastal storm that impacts most of Maine. The combined Gulf of Mexico and Atlantic (Hatteras) track will usually produce the classic nor'easter. A combined track storm has three potential causes. The first scenario is typical for the Gulf of Mexico track. In this case, a storm forms in the Gulf of Mexico with movement directly up the eastern seaboard toward Maine. The second scenario is a storm that initially forms in the Gulf of Mexico, but the central low-pressure seems to "jump" farther along the eastern coast while intensifying greatly. The third is a classic scenario in nor'easter development. The process begins with one storm moving across the Great Lakes (possibly an Alberta Clipper) or moving up the Ohio River Valley toward New England. This storm begins to dissipate, transferring its energy to another storm forming off the Mid-Atlantic coast. The second storm then becomes the primary storm and may strengthen to a very intense coastal storm wreaking havoc along the entire eastern seaboard.

El Niño—Southern Oscillation (ENSO)

During the winter of 1997–98 it seemed like every weather event around the world was being blamed on the very strong El Niño of that winter. Although many events cannot be blamed solely on the presence of El Niño conditions, the impact of a strong event such as the one in 1997–98 or in 1982–83 can be very far reaching. As a result, the term El Niño has become prominent in the vocabulary of everyday forecasters, as it is responsible for specific weather conditions during years when it develops.

El Niño (EN) is one extreme in a series of atmospheric and oceanic conditions in the Pacific Ocean that is referred to as the Southern Oscillation (SO), hence the overall acronym of ENSO. Considering that the Pacific Ocean occupies about a third of the surface of the earth, it is not surprising that major fluctuations in the characteristics of that ocean will impact many parts of the world. The term El Niño comes from the Spanish name of the Christ child because the peak of El Niño conditions is felt around Christmas along the South American coastline, the area where the presence of this phenomenon was first identified by the fishermen of Peru long before it came into vogue in our modern-day weather culture. The opposite extreme in the oscillation is referred to as La Niña, but there are also times when neither El Niño nor La Niña conditions are prevalent. A rather "tongue-in-cheek" expression of this situation has been coined "La Nada" by some individuals.

An El Niño event is characterized by a weakening of the northeast trade winds in the equatorial Pacific Ocean. The weakened winds allow the warm waters near Australia to migrate eastward toward South America, squelching the current of cold Antarctic water along the western South American coast. This limits productivity of smaller organisms and disrupts the overall food chain, resulting in a poor catch by Peruvian fishermen—the reason they were well aware of El Niño even before modern climatologists and meteorologists realized its global significance. This lessening of the strength of the trade winds and the migration of warm water to the east also produces a characteristic pattern in global winter circulation systems. In the Northern Hemisphere a very strong subtropical jet stream crosses the southern United States, resulting in increased storm activity along the California coast and in the southeastern U. S. At the same time, the average position of the polar jet stream shifts northward, allowing a warm airflow into most of the northern tier of the country, including Maine. Winters across the northern U. S., particularly in the center of the country, will tend to be warmer than normal. While this is the case for Maine, the warming is usually not as consistent or as great in the state compared to more central parts of the country.

The nature of a La Niña event is opposite that of the El Niño. In the case of a La Niña, the easterly trade winds strengthen and the warm pool of water in the equatorial Pacific is pushed farther west. The cold current along the South American coast is very much pronounced, yet winter global circulation patterns are still modified by these conditions. The effect in the United States is usually a very prevalent blocking high-pressure system over the eastern Pacific Ocean, producing a large ridge in the upper-air wind patterns over the western U. S. There may be a slight trough in the east, but its position may often be to the north, meaning still the likelihood of a warmer than average winter in Maine. As with El Niño, any wintertime warming associated with La Niña is not consistent from year to year, nor is the magnitude of the warming. Consequently, the impact of ENSO on Maine is the possibility of warmer winters, but this trend is not as consistent as in other parts of the country. Other forcing factors should play a more significant role in shaping our weather in years when the ENSO condition is neutral.

North Atlantic Oscillation (NAO)

One way scientists characterize circulation patterns in the North Atlantic is the North Atlantic Oscillation, or NAO. This is the difference between the central pressure of the Icelandic Low and the central pressure of the Bermuda High. It is calculated by subtracting the surface pressure at Stykkisholmur, Iceland, (representative of the pressure of the Icelandic Low) from the surface pressure recorded at Lisbon, Portugal (representative of the pressure of the Bermuda High). The difference between the two determines whether the NAO is in the positive mode or the negative mode The positive mode results when the pressure difference between the two systems is very large, while a very small difference indicates the negative mode. The result of the different modes of the NAO is reflected in upper-air patterns in the North Atlantic region and the Northern Hemisphere (Fig. 3.4). Because the mode of the NAO has far reaching effects away from the two pressure systems in the North Atlantic it is referred to as a teleconnection pattern, meaning that its effect is transported over great distances. Although climatologists and other atmospheric scientists have been aware of the NAO and its impact for several decades, it is now being used much more frequently by forecasters to explain to the general public why certain weather conditions may exist in an area like Maine.

The NAO has the greatest impact on Maine's weather during the winter months. When the NAO is in the positive mode, the great difference in pressure between the Icelandic Low and Bermuda High produces a very strong zonal pattern to the jet stream (Fig. 3.4), bringing relatively mild temperatures and a less active storm pattern to Maine. On the other hand, when the NAO is in the negative mode, the very small pressure difference helps a strong blocking high form over Greenland, which often remains in place for several weeks to months. This is a long time when you consider that many weather systems move across the U. S. in just a few days. Once this blocking high becomes established over Greenland, the resulting jet stream pattern to the west turns into a very pronounced meridional pattern (Fig. 3.4). A trough will become very prevalent over the eastern U. S. with cold air encroaching into this part of the country. The air over the east is also much colder than both the warmer ocean water off the east coast and the air mass over the ocean, leading to the formation of many storm systems that move up the eastern limb of the trough. These storms are classic coastal storms, or nor'easters, that may bring large snowfalls to Maine and other parts of the eastern United States. The NAO seems to operate on a multi-decadal time frame, meaning that the positive mode will be more prevalent over a 20-year time frame, then the negative mode will be more prevalent over the next 20 years.

Volcanic Eruptions

It may be hard to believe that a natural event halfway around the world could affect Maine's weather and climate. However, this is exactly what can happen with some volcanic eruptions. When you look at a video or pictures of an eruption, it may seem obvious that the great amounts of ash and gases put high into the atmosphere would have some impact on the weather. The most likely effect is volcanic winter, a cooling of the earth's surface because the material injected into the atmosphere blocks incoming solar radiation. The extent and duration of the cooling depends on the nature of the eruption. The ash that is injected high into the atmosphere will block sunlight, but the individual ash particles are large enough that they do not remain in the air for a long period of time and they do not travel great distances in a large enough quantity to have far-reaching effects. Consequently, any cooling from the ash produced by an eruption is short-lived and limited to areas very close to the erupting volcano.

The part of an eruption that would affect Maine's weather is the gas produced. More specifically, sulfur gas produced by an eruption has the potential to modify Maine's climate and that of the entire globe by cooling surface temperatures. Many gases are too soluble to remain aloft for very long and settle out very quickly. Sulfur-rich gases, on the other hand, are not as soluble and convert to tiny droplets of sulfuric acid via reactions with water and other chemical compounds in the atmosphere. These droplets both absorb and reflect incoming solar radiation, cooling the earth's surface. This process will only occur to the extent needed to cool the climate if these acidic droplets form in the stratosphere, the layer above the troposphere—where our weather forms—because droplets that form in the troposphere will be quickly washed-out by precipitation. Since no precipitation forms in the stratosphere, the sulfuric acid particles can remain there for several years as the only way they settle out is by gravity. The most recent eruption whose material had sufficient sulfur content and was ejected with enough force to propel it into the stratosphere was the 1991 Mt. Pinatubo, Philippines, eruption (Fig. 3.7). The "Year Without a Summer" of 1816 was most likely caused by the 1815 eruption of Mt. Tambora, in Indonesia. It is noteworthy that the United States

Figure 3.7. Photograph of the eruption of Mt. Pinatubo, Philippines, 1991. Photo from the National Oceanic and Atmospheric Administration.

eruption of Mt. St. Helens in 1980 was very explosive, but did not contain much sulfur, thus it did not have a long-term effect on climate.

There is another factor that determines the extent of climatic cooling associated with a volcanic eruption. That is the location of the volcano relative to global circulation patterns. Because there is an overall equator-to-pole movement of air, material from volcanoes in equatorial zones will be distributed to both the northern and southern hemispheres. This results in global cooling. If the volcano erupts in the mid- or high latitudes of either hemisphere, the material will primarily remain in the hemisphere where the volcano is located and global cooling will be greatly lessened. There is very little exchange of air between the Northern and Southern Hemispheres.

How much cooling are we actually talking about, and how long will it last after a volcanic eruption? In general, the amount of global cooling following a major eruption is on the order of 0.5°F (~1.0°C) during the first and second years following the eruption. In the case of larger eruptions, there may be identifiable cooling for another two years, although of much less magnitude than the previous two years. In areas like Maine, the most noticeable cooling is observed during the summer following the eruption. Many shopkeepers along the coast may remember the very cool summer and poor tourist season of 1992 following the 1991 Mt. Pinatubo eruption.

There can also be conflicting factors that affect the climatic impact of an eruption. This was the case following the 1982 eruption of El Chichón, in Mexico. That eruption had the potential to cool our climate, but there was a very strong El Niño event that winter, resulting in much less cooling than expected over wide areas of the Northern Hemisphere.

Greenhouse Gases

One of the most talked about controls on our present weather and climate is the abundance of greenhouse gases in our atmosphere. The most common is carbon dioxide (CO_2), with recent increases caused by the burning of fossil fuels. Other gases also contribute to the greenhouse effect, including methane (CH_4) and even water vapor (H_2O). Interestingly, water vapor is actually a much more effective greenhouse gas than carbon dioxide. The term greenhouse effect originates from the manner in which a greenhouse works to keep plants warmer than the outside environment. Solar radiation penetrates into a greenhouse and it is reflected outward. The radiation reflected outward is termed long-wave radiation. However, the glass in the greenhouse prevents the long-wave radiation from escaping, thereby heating up the greenhouse. Gases such as CO_2, CH_4, and H_2O act like the glass in a greenhouse by keeping long-wave radiation in the troposphere, heating the earth's surface. Ironically, the earth was able to become habitable for life due to the presence of greenhouse gases in the early stages of the earth's formation.

The Sun

The sun of course also exerts a major control on our climate. At one time the sun's energy output was thought to be constant—the term solar constant was used to describe the solar radiation that reaches the earth's atmosphere. We now know that the output of the sun does vary and over the last few hundred years there have been times when that output has decreased. This decrease is reflected in the amount of sunspot activity, a lower number of sunspots coinciding with lower solar output and cooler temperatures. There were three distinct periods over the last 1000 years when low sunspot activity is known to have occurred. The last period of low activity was the Maunder Minimum, which occurred from 1645 to 1715. These periods are characterized by overall cooler temperatures, not only in the northeastern United States, but also globally. We are presently in a period of high sunspot activity, which may be making some contribution to our current warmer conditions compared to the past several hundred years.

Randomness

I have summarized many of the factors that influence our everyday weather and longer-term climatic conditions. Unfortunately, there are times when none of these factors seem to play a major role in controlling the conditions that will prevail in Maine over several weeks, months, or even years. Basically, our weather also has a random component to it, with no distinct or identifiable control influencing the conditions we observe. In such a case, circulation patterns may favor specific conditions, like colder than average temperatures, but there is no specific reason why such a pattern may exist. For instance, there may not have been a recent volcanic eruption or the NAO is not in a mode favorable for a persistent northwest flow into Maine, but a cold northwest flow is dominant nonetheless. No wonder forecasting can be so complicated, particularly in an area like Maine, which is influenced by mountains, ocean, multiple storm tracks, and various aspects of global circulation patterns like the NAO or an El Niño event.

4

WHERE THE NUMBERS COME FROM

You'll see throughout this book, many maps and tables showing temperature and precipitation values, among other types of weather and climatic data, for many cities and towns around the state. You may be asking, "Where do the numbers come from?" or "What does normal mean when the television forecaster says today was 5°F above normal?" Perhaps you're wondering who actually makes the weather forecasts we hear everyday in Maine.

The information presented in this book comes from several different sources, but most was collected through various programs in the National Oceanic and Atmospheric Administration (NOAA), a part of the United States Department of Commerce. The programs responsible for collecting the data at the various sites around the state are under the auspices of the National Weather Service (NWS), which is part of NOAA. The data collected fall under essentially three different categories, or levels, from 73 climate stations in the state of Maine (Fig. 4.1). The total number of stations is not definitive because some stations have been collecting data continuously for a long period of time and continue to do so, others have only been collecting this information for a short time, some collected information for an extended period but no longer, and some only collected data for a few years sometime in the past. Several stations in the state were established in the 1800s following-up on the weather records kept at some of Maine's forts in the early 1800s. A group of modern stations was established in the 1920s, another group in 1948. Since then, various stations have been added to the list, with the greatest number being added in the early 1970s. Although there are more than 100 years of records from some stations, this length of time is not very long from a true climatic perspective.

The most complete data collected are at the two first-order stations in the state, located at the NWS office in Caribou and at the Portland International Jetport. Hourly readings for temperature, precipitation, barometric pressure, dew point, relative humidity, wind direction and speed, sky conditions, visibility, and general weather conditions are recorded at these sites. However, most weather and climatic data for the state, and the United States as a whole, come from the Co-op Volunteer Network run by the NWS. Individuals collect basic information at these sites, which include both private residences and public facilities, using instrumentation provided by the NWS (Fig. 4.1). The data basically summarize the predominant conditions for the day, including maximum and minimum temperature, total precipitation (including water equivalent of all snow), snowfall, and snow depth. Some stations may only collect total precipitation and snowfall data. A third source of data comes from the automatic weather stations (ASOS) now established at airports around the state. Unfortunately, in some cases, these automatic weather stations have replaced the readings collected by individuals at the airports, which has led to some controversy about the consistency of the data. There have been some problems in the reliability of the data collected by automatic weather stations, as determined elsewhere in the U. S. via comparisons of their numbers with those of a nearby co-op station. Nevertheless, the ASOS network provides daily summaries of temperature, precipitation, dew point, relative humidity, wind speed and direction, and barometric pressure.

In 2002–03, two other data sites were established in Maine as part of the United States Climate Reference Network (USCRN). This program was established by NOAA to evaluate future climate change by eliminating several potential problems with existing climatic data collected throughout the country. The problems the USCRN hopes to eliminate include changes in the instrumentation used to collect climatic data, stations being moved sometime during their history, and changes in land use surrounding the collecting site and the encroachment of urbanized areas—a particular problem for existing climatic stations resulting in an increase in temperature caused by such things as black-topped parking lots. All of these circumstances can jeopardize a reliable evaluation of changes in climate using the existing instrumental data that are available. Consequently, NOAA is establishing sites around the country that will remain in the same place with instrumentation that will not change and in areas that are unlikely to be affected by changes in land use adjacent to the station. The two existing sites in Maine are in Old Town and Limestone (Fig. 4.2). Real-time data from these stations are available online at www.ncdc. gov/oa/climate/uscrn. Data collected at these two sites include temperature, precipitation, relative humidity, dew point, wind speed, and solar radiation.

Once volunteers at individual sites collect data, the information is passed on to the appropriate NWS offices, which then forward it to the National Climatic Data Center (NCDC) in Asheville, North Carolina. NCDC does a check for quality control and quality assurance before the data are available to the general public. The data are commonly available in either daily or monthly summary formats and, in the case of precipitation data, sometimes in hourly or 15-minute formats. This information is available online at www.ncdc.gov.

Despite the existence of climatic data for the many stations across Maine (former and ongoing), there is always the potential for problems within individual data sets, such as a moved station, as was the case in Bangor in 1953, when the present station was estab-

Figure 4.1. Photographs of co-op weather station at Sebec Lake. Photograph on the right taken on the day of the record minimum temperature of -43°F on January 20 and 21, 1994. Photos courtesy of Bill Larrabee, observer at the Sebec Lake station, who appears in the right photograph.

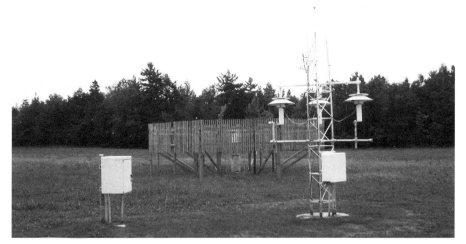

Figure 4.2. Photograph of the Climate Reference Network station located at Rogers Farm, University of Maine. Photo from Greg Zielinski.

Table 4.1. Historical Climatology Network Stations in Maine and Time Period Covered

Station	ID Number	Time Period Covered
Acadia National Park	170100	1885-Present
Eastport	172426	1833-Present
Farmington	172765	1889-Present
Gardiner	173406	1837-Present
Houlton	174944	1835-Present
Lewiston	174566	1886-Present
Millinocket	175304	1903-Present
Orono	176430	1869-Present
Portland	176905	1837-Present
Presque Isle	176937	1909-Present
Ripogenus Dam	177174	1925-Present
Woodland	179891	1917-Present

Note: Station ID numbers as shown on Figure 4.3. The time period covered may have gaps and not all parameters may have been collected over the entire length of the record, particularly for sites beginning in the 1830s (except Portland).

lished at the airport. To take into account such problems, the Historical Climate Network (HCN) was established by NOAA (Table 4.1). The difference between the HCN station records and other records from around the state is that the data collected for the 12 HCN stations in Maine have been adjusted to take into account various parameters that may jeopardize the accuracy of the original data. These parameters may include station moves, impact from urbanization, and potential bias introduced by the time of day observations are recorded. Various factors have been applied to the original data based on numerous studies by climatologists to evaluate such problems. It is believed that these 12 stations may provide the longest and most continuous records for the state of Maine.

Temperature and precipitation data from the co-op network are averaged to produce the normal ranges you hear about on forecasts and in the daily weather report. However, the daily, monthly, seasonal, or annual averages that are cited when compared to the actual values for a particular day or for the corresponding time frame do not come from the complete data set available for a single station. Normals reported by the NWS and subsequently used by most radio and television forecasters are based on 30-year averages that are updated every ten years. For example, the climatic norms used during the period from 2001 to 2010 are based on the 30-year averages for the time period from 1971 to 2000. There are 61 stations around the state that have been used to calculate the norms. The previous ten-year period (1991–2000) used the 30-year averages from 1961 to 1990. This process enables us to compare existing records with the most recent climatic conditions. Most of the figures presented here are based on the 1971–2000 normals because,

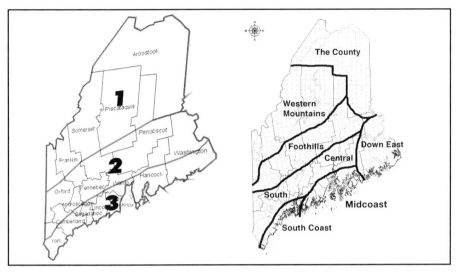

Figure 4.3. Climate divisions of Maine as used by the National Climatic Data Center (left) and as defined in this book (right).

for the first time, the NCDC has calculated normals by adjusting the readings for any influence from urbanization and for the time observations were taken.

Statewide averages, on the other hand, are not calculated by simply averaging together all the stations in the state, but are based on the averages for the climatic divisions of Maine. These averages are available beginning in 1895 and extending to the present. The NCDC has broken down every state into a series of regions that are climatically very similar as a way to account for the variability across many of the states, particularly the larger ones. Maine has been divided into three climatic divisions with Division 1 being the Northern Division, Division 2 the South Central Division, and Division 3 the Coastal Division (Fig. 4.3). Once monthly or annual temperature or precipitation averages are determined for each of the three divisions, they are adjusted to account for the area of the state covered by each division and then summed to get a statewide average. Division 1 comprises 54% of the state, Division 2 covers 31% of the state, and Division 3 only covers 15% of the area of the state. For example, if the average January temperature for 1895–2007 for Division 1 is 11.4°F, for Division 2 is 17.0°F, and for Division 3 is 21.2°F, then the average temperature for January in Maine is 11.4(0.54) + 17.0(0.31) + 21.2(0.15) = 14.6°F. Given that more than half the state is contained within Division 1, climatic trends in the state are dominated by changes in the northern division. Potential problems with this methodology and with how new stations are averaged into all calculations are discussed more in Chapter 14. For this book, I have broken down the climatic divisions into regions of greater similarity than those put forth by the NCDC divisions (Fig. 4.3).

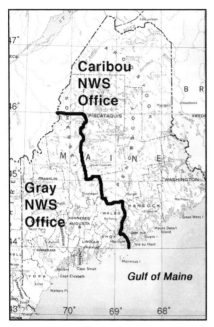

Figure 4.4. Parts of Maine covered by each of the two National Weather Service Forecast Offices in Maine.

Figure 4.5. Photographs of the Gray National Weather Service Forecasting Office (top), a weather balloon about to be launched (lower left), and the radar facility (lower right). Photos courtesy of Hendricus Lulofs and the Caribou NWS.

Daily forecasts for Maine come from the two National Weather Service Forecast Offices (NWSFO), one located in Caribou and the other in Gray (Fig. 4.4). The Caribou office provides forecasts and issues severe weather watches and warnings for most of northern and eastern Maine, while the Gray office provides the same services for most of southern and western Maine. The Gray office also serves most of New Hampshire. In addition to providing forecasts, these offices are very involved in educating school children and the general public on various interesting and informative aspects of our weather. Both offices also provide forecasts for marine interests in the Gulf of Maine from Eastport to Merrimack, Massachusetts, with the help of data available from buoys located in the gulf. Radar facilities are available at each station, and both sites release weather balloons twice a day to collect upper air information that goes into computer models for forecasting weather patterns in the United States and around the world (Fig. 4.5).

5

TEMPERATURE

Temperature is perhaps the one aspect of Maine's weather that draws the most interest and attention in everyday life. The most obvious reasons for wondering what the temperature will be are to address such questions as, "what do I wear today, how should I dress the children, particularly as they wait for the school bus, and do I need to take a jacket with me to work?" During certain times of the year, other questions of concern related to the temperature include, "must I cover the plants tonight," as that first frost is always a telltale sign of winter's approach, and "will it be hot enough to go to the beach or the lake today, or over the weekend?" No doubt about it, temperature dictates many, many aspects of our lives.

■ WHAT CONTROLS MAINE'S TEMPERATURE?

Generally speaking, two dominant factors dictate what the temperature will be at any one place in the state. Simply put, they are the amount of direct sunshine reaching the surface and the direction of the wind. The amount of sunshine received at any one place is actually determined by many different factors. One obvious factor is the timing within the calendar year, that is, the season. The tilt of the earth and its orbit result in more daylight and potential sunshine per 24-hour period in the northern hemisphere during the summer than in the winter. Areas in Maine receive more than 15 hours of daylight on the summer solstice or within a day of the first day of summer (Table 5.1). There is about a 30-minute difference between northern parts of the state, for example Fort Kent, and the southernmost town, Kittery. Kittery receives 15 hours, 22 minutes of daylight on June 21, and the amount of daylight gradually increases as you move northward. Fort Kent receives around 15 hours, 56 minutes of daylight on June 21 (Table 5.1). The opposite

Table 5.1. Amount of Daylight on the 21st of Each Month for Various Towns in Maine

Town	Jan	Feb	Mar	Apr	May	Jun	Jul	Aug	Sep	Oct	Nov	Dec
Augusta	9:25	10:45	12:13	13:46	15:00	15:32	15:00	13:44	12:13	10:42	9:24	8:51
Bangor	9:21	10:34	12:13	13:48	15:04	15:36	15:03	13:46	12:13	10:41	9:20	8:47
Bar Harbor	9:24	10:45	12:14	13:47	15:01	15:32	15:00	13:45	12:12	10:42	9:23	8:50
Bethel	9:25	10:45	12:13	13:47	15:02	15:32	15:01	13:44	12:12	10:42	9:22	8:47
Caribou	9:11	10:38	12:15	13:56	15:18	15:52	15:18	13:53	12:13	10:34	9:08	8:31
Dover-Foxcroft	9:19	10:42	12:14	13:50	15:06	15:39	15:06	13:47	12:13	10:40	9:18	8:45
Eastport	9:21	10:44	12:13	13:48	15:04	15:36	15:04	13:47	12:13	10:40	9:20	8:47
Farmington	9:22	10:45	12:14	13:47	15:03	15:35	15:03	13:45	12:12	10:41	9:21	8:48
Fort Kent	9:07	10:37	12:14	13:58	15:21	15:56	15:21	13:55	12:13	10:33	9:05	8:28
Houlton	9:14	10:40	12:14	13:53	15:13	15:46	15:31	13:50	12:13	10:37	9:12	8:38
Jackman	9:17	10:42	12:14	13:52	15:09	15:42	15:08	13:49	12:13	10:38	9:15	8:31
Kennebunk	9:30	10:48	12:13	13:43	14:54	15:24	14:54	13:41	12:13	10:45	9:28	8:57
Kittery	9:32	10:48	12:13	13:42	14:53	15:22	14:52	13:39	12:11	10:46	9:30	8:59
Lewiston	9:26	10:46	12:14	13:46	14:59	15:30	14:58	13:43	12:12	10:42	9:25	8:52
Machias	9:22	10:44	12:14	13:48	15:03	15:35	15:02	13:45	12:12	10:41	9:21	8:48
Millinocket	9:17	10:41	12:14	13:52	15:09	15:53	15:09	13:49	12:13	10:38	9:15	8:41
Portland	9:29	10:47	12:13	13:44	14:56	15:26	14:56	13:42	12:12	10:44	9:27	8:55
Presque Isle	9:30	10:48	12:13	13:43	14:54	15:24	14:54	13:41	12:12	10:45	9:28	8:57
Rangeley	9:20	10:43	12:14	13:49	15:05	15:37	15:04	13:46	12:12	10:40	9:19	8:46
Sanford	9:29	10:48	12:13	13:44	14:54	15:25	14:55	13:41	12:12	10:45	9:28	8:57
Vanceboro	9:18	10:42	12:14	13:41	15:09	15:31	15:08	13:49	12:12	10:38	9:15	8:42
Waterville	9:24	10:45	12:14	13:47	15:02	15:33	15:01	13:45	12:12	10:42	9:22	8:50

Note: Number of hours: minutes shown is for 2004. Amount for other years may vary slightly. Calculated from data provided by the Office of Naval Research at www.onr.navy.mil.

trend holds true for the winter, with the state receiving fewer than nine hours of daylight on the winter solstice—December 21. In this case, Fort Kent only receives 8 hours, 28 minutes of daylight at the beginning of winter, while Kittery receives 8 hours, 59 minutes of daylight (Table 5.1). The amount of daylight increases from northern to southern Maine during the winter, the opposite trend to that observed during the summer. Hours of daylight on the spring and fall equinox are about half way between the winter and summer extremes, that is, the state receives about 12 hours of daylight on the equinox, on average (Table 5.1).

In addition to the difference in the amount of available daylight, and the potential for sunshine with the seasons, the effectiveness of the solar radiation reaching the surface changes with the seasons. The ability of the sun's rays to heat the earth's surface decreases in the winter as the sun is at a much lower angle in the sky (Fig. 5.1). During the summer,

Figure 5.1. Reflection of the sun's rays showing that, even at high noon, the sun is only about 20° above the horizon in late Decemeber. This photographer is taking advantage of the interesting photo opportunities produced by the low angle of the sun along Otter Cliffs, Acadia National Park. Photo by Greg Zielinski.

the sun is higher in the sky, thus the sun's rays are much more effective in heating the surface. As an example, think about how the light beam from a flashlight held immediately overhead is able to be concentrated in the diameter of the light itself. When the flashlight is tilted, the same amount of light reaches the surface, but it covers much more area. In the latter case, the heat is distributed over a greater area, resulting in lower temperatures. This is the case for winter in Maine, and the Northern Hemisphere as a whole.

The next obvious control on the amount of sunshine that reaches the surface is cloud cover. Cloud cover has two opposite effects on temperature. During daylight hours, the thicker the clouds, the less of the sun's radiation that reaches the surface, and the lower the resulting temperature. On average, Maine only receives about 50% of the available sunshine because of frequent cloud cover. The reason for the abundance of clouds is partly a function of where Maine is located compared to the major storm tracks and airflow in the Northern Hemisphere. Clouds that form during a summer afternoon are frequently a direct result of surface heating. Air near the surface is heated, rises, and as it rises it cools. Once the temperature of this rising air is cool enough for water vapor to condense, clouds begin to form. Increased heating of the land surface causes greater cloud development, eventually helping to reduce surface temperature by blocking sunlight.

The other impact cloud cover has on temperature occurs at night. Without a cloud cover, all the daytime heat is lost once the sun sets. This loss of heat to the atmosphere is

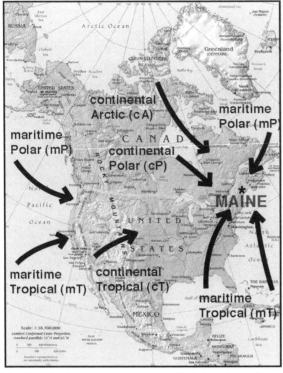

Figure 5.2. Major air masses across North America and those that have the greatest effect on Maine's weather and climate. See text for details.

referred to as radiational cooling. That is why the coldest temperatures overnight occur under clear, calm conditions. If there is too much wind, the air is stirred up and the temperature at the surface will not cool as much as when it is calm. When there is a cloud cover at night, the daytime heat is not lost to the atmosphere and nighttime temperatures will not fall as much as under clear conditions.

A less obvious factor that controls the amount of solar radiation reaching the surface, and thus the temperature, is the presence of aerosols in the atmosphere. Aerosols are small liquid or solid particles suspended in a gaseous medium, such as the atmosphere. One of the most influential aerosols may be the material from volcanic eruptions. The sulfuric acid droplets produced from an eruption will both reflect and absorb incoming solar radiation. Other aerosols, such as those that make up smog can also play a role in temperature by their ability to keep in heat at night, much like cloud cover.

The wind is the second overall major control on Maine's temperature primarily because its prevalent direction brings air masses into Maine that dictate the resulting temperature distribution across the state. The characteristics of an air mass reflect the area from which the air originated, and there are three primary air masses that often move into Maine (Fig. 5.2). One prevalent air mass arrives from northwest Canada, although, during the winter, air sometimes comes across the North Pole from Siberia. This air mass can be cold or very cold depending on the season it arrives in Maine. The second major air mass that often covers the state originates south to southwest of the state. This air is warm to hot and often humid as it frequently comes from the Gulf of Mexico or the subtropical portion of the Atlantic Ocean. The third most common air mass affecting Maine comes off the northern Atlantic, usually arriving on northeast winds. This air is generally cool and humid.

A third control that exerts a noticeable influence on our temperature is the ocean.

Large bodies of water like the Gulf of Maine have a significant buffering affect on climate. Water does not gain or lose heat as quickly as landmasses do, thus areas adjacent to the Gulf of Maine will not be as hot during the summer, and they will not be as cold during the winter. Interestingly, the effect of the ocean on Maine's climate, and especially on temperature, does not reach as far inland as one may think. In fact, most of the state is dominated by airflow from across the continent, not off the ocean. The result is that the state has a high degree of continentality and temperatures across most interior parts of the state reflect this situation.

■ TEMPERATURE DISTRIBUTION

Mean annual temperature (MAT) varies from a minimum of around 36°F in the far northwest part of the state (Allagash region) to slightly over 46°F in the southwestern part of the state (around Sanford; Fig. 5.3). These numbers produce a MAT of 41.2°F for the state. This 10°F north-south difference in only 300 miles is quite dramatic, and it is one of the notoriety's of Maine's weather and climate. In fact, if you consider that the MAT in the Allagash region is just 4°F above freezing, it is no wonder that Mainers are hearty souls.

Seasonal contrasts in temperature can be quite dramatic, with the greatest contrast occurring between the extreme seasons of winter and summer. The coldest day of the year will often occur during either of two time periods during the winter, although there is some variability across the state. A large number of stations will reach their lowest temperature of the year in mid-January, often on the 17th. A slightly greater number of stations reach their lowest on February 7. The average coldest minimum temperature for the state is approximately -16°F around Allagash and Van Buren. On the other hand, the hottest day of the year usually centers on

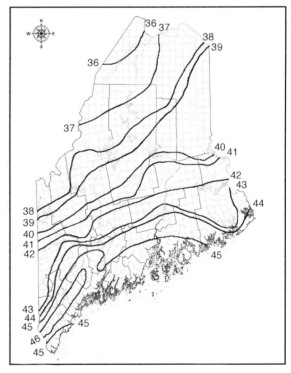

Figure 5.3. Mean annual temperature across the state of Maine. Contour lines interpolated between existing climatic stations.

Figure 5.4. Average monthly
temperature for the state of Maine.

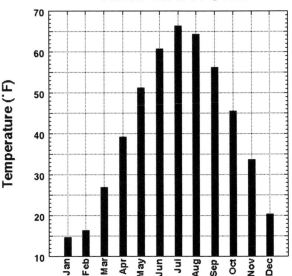

AVERAGE MONTHLY TEMPERATURE

the 18th and 19th of July, with most stations reaching their maximum on either of those two days. The average maximum temperature for the state is 81°F, measured at Sanford. This great seasonal variability is also reflected in the daily average seasonal temperatures for the state as a whole and for the various climatic regions within the state.

■ DEGREE DAYS

The concept of degree-days was created during the energy crisis of the 1970s. Its purpose is to provide an easily comparable number for estimating how much you would have to heat or cool your house during the appropriate season to remain comfortable. Heating degree-days (HDD) is a measure of how much heating, and thus, the likely amount of oil or gas consumption will be needed for adequate heating. Ultimately, year-to-year comparisons may be made to evaluate a household's or business's trend in energy consumption. Cooling degree days (CDD) are used for evaluating how much energy is needed for summer cooling, such as running an air conditioner. Individuals in cooler climates, like Maine, are obviously much more concerned with HDD numbers than CDD numbers.

Degree-days are calculated using a base temperature of 65°F, meaning that when average daily temperatures are below 65°F, HDD will be accumulated and when daily temperatures are above 65°F then CDD will be accumulated. For example, if the average

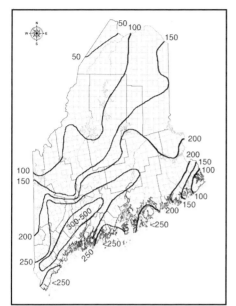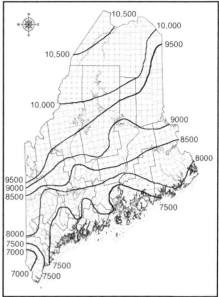

Figure 5.5. Average annual Cooling Degree Days (CDD; left) and Heating Degree Days (HDD; right) for the state of Maine.

daily temperature on September 1 was 63°F then 2 HDD would be accrued. Let's say a cold front then moved through late that night, leading to an average daily temperature of 55°F on September 2. That would mean that 10 HDD were compiled for the 2nd, and the running total for the month of September would be 12 after the first two days. Degree-days are cumulative throughout each month and the year. If the daily temperature for the 3rd of September quickly jumped to 68°F with passage of a fast-moving warm front, then 3 CDD would be compiled for the 3rd, so it is possible to accumulate both HDD and CDD during a single month, particularly during fall and spring. Interestingly, in Maine, HDD are accumulated somewhere in the state during every month of the year, yet CDD are only accumulated from May through September (Fig. 5.5).

Heating degree-days range from 7000 to 10,500 from south to north across the state, with a statewide average of 8579 (Fig. 5.5). Cooling degree-days, on the other hand, range from 50 to 500, with an average of only 195 for the state. The greatest numbers of CDD are found in the southern interior and central parts of the state, as the cooling effect of the sea breeze keeps temperatures down along the coast. It is no wonder that air conditioners are not an essential household item in the state. Mainers may gripe a bit during those few hot and humid days during the summer when an air conditioner would be nice, but they usually tough it out.

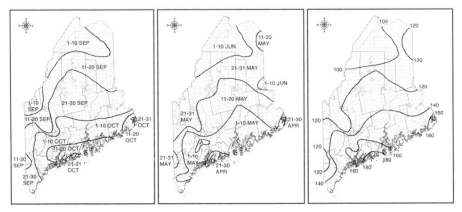

Figure 5.6. Average time range for the first frost (based on 32°F) of fall (left), last frost of spring (center), and length of growing season based on annual frost timing for the state of Maine.

■ FROST, FREEZE, AND GROWING SEASON

As temperatures begin to cool during early fall, many farmers—including people with home gardens—begin to keep an eye on nighttime temperatures as that first frost of the season looms. These same people are cautious during late spring as they worry about protecting their young plants from a late frost. The growing season is based on the last and first frosts, that is, the date of the last occurrence of 32°F in the spring and the date of the first occurrence of 32°F in the fall. The number of days in between those dates makes up the growing season.

Although the 32°F temperature is used for consistency in noting the timing of frost and the growing season, that temperature alone does not necessarily mean a frost will occur at a given place. Strong winds that may accompany a 32°F night will mix the air and prevent the accumulation of condensed water vapor on plant surfaces, preventing a frost cover. There are also so many local conditions affecting temperature and in many cases a frost can be localized, but this depends on the microclimate of an area. For instance, a garden that is relatively close to a house may not quite reach that 32°F mark, even though most of the area around it will. Heat emanating from the house may keep the temperature in the garden just above freezing. Abundant tree cover close to an area can also help keep nighttime heat in by reducing the amount of radiational cooling. As you drive past open fields, however, the frost-covered pumpkins may be evident. Proximity to a body of water may also reduce the potential for frost to occur. Cold air that settles into valleys at night provides one of the greatest variations in local frost timing. It may not take much of a hollow in the landscape to pool enough cold air for temperatures to reach 32°F compared to the surrounding area. It is for these reasons that the average first and last frosts for Maine, as well as the length of growing season, are only general averages (Fig. 5.6).

The timing of the first frost in the fall across the state spans a two-month period from early September in northwestern-most Maine to late October in some areas of the

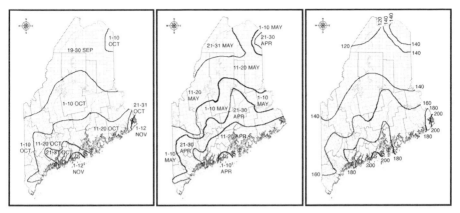

Figure 5.7. Average time range for the first freeze (based on 28°F) of fall (left), last freeze of spring (center), and length of freeze-free season (in days) based on annual freeze timing for the state of Maine.

coast and Down East (Fig. 5.6). There can be quite a bit of variability in the date of first frost from year to year. In fact, it is not uncommon for the first frost to occur in late August in the northern part of the state, particularly during summers that are cooler than average. That makes for some cold mornings as late-summer vacationers wake next to their favorite trout stream. On the other hand, that first frost may not occur until the middle of November in southern and coastal areas of the state.

Overall, the northwest to southeast trend in warmth across the state is not unexpected given the effect of the ocean on temperatures during the cold season. There is evidence, however, of frosts occurring one to two weeks earlier in the western part of the state compared to the same latitude in central and eastern parts. These earlier frosts are most likely due to cold air settling in the western valleys where the climatic stations are predominantly located. Farmington, for example, is quite chilly given its relative north-south setting in the state. Add a little elevation from the overall hilly terrain, and the recipe is right for early frosts.

The last frost of the season generally occurs in late April in the immediate coastal areas of the state as well as in the more urban areas of Lewiston and Augusta. Frost dates from the cities reflect the idea of an urban microclimate, as rural areas surrounding these two cities may have their last frost up to two weeks later. Consequently, most areas in the southern part of the state have their last frost in early May, while northwestern areas will frequently have their last frost the first week of June. The timing of the last frost in relation to location is not quite as variable as that of the first frost. On average, the timing of the last frost spans about a month (early May–early June) across the state. Microclimates do play a great role in the actual timing of frost and this is reflected in the small pockets of later or earlier last frosts for some towns compared to surrounding areas. For instance, Danforth, on the New Brunswick border, usually has its last frost in early June compared to late May for most of the rest of that part of the state; and Caribou's last frost appears to be a bit early compared to its surrounding area.

Given the average first and last frost dates, the length of the growing season across the state ranges from fewer than 100 days in the extreme northwest to a more than 180 days in the midcoast area (Fig. 5.6). Those numbers translate to only about a 3-month growing season from around Clayton Lake and Squa Pan Dam northward to the Allagash region, but up to a 5- or 6-month season around Port Clyde, upward toward the Lewiston and Augusta areas, and around Eastport. Most of the state, however, falls into the 100–160-day range (3 to 5 months), thus an overall variability of about two months across the state. The short growing season does not lead to many opportunities for a great variety in crop production, as vegetables such as broccoli, cauliflower, and tomatoes require 120–150 days. Corn, cucumbers, and carrots, on the other hand need only 60–90 days. It is no wonder that the bounty from home gardens is much appreciated by Mainers.

Although the length of growing season is often determined by the number of days between the last and first frosts, the presence of frost does not necessarily mean the death of a plant. In fact, there are three levels for characterizing the severity of a frost. Temperatures between 32° and 29°F cause a light freeze, which can kill tender plants, but have little destructive effect on other vegetation (Koss et al., 1988). Heavy damage to fruit blossoms and to tender and semi-hardy plants occurs when temperatures fall between 25° and 28°F (Koss et al., 1988). This is a moderate freeze; therefore, the most critical temperature for most agricultural concerns is 28°F. Consequently, for the purpose of summarizing trends in the potential critical impact of cold temperatures on agriculture, the freeze-free period is calculated by determining the number of days between the average last 28°F occurrence in the spring and the first 28°F occurrence in the fall. Temper-

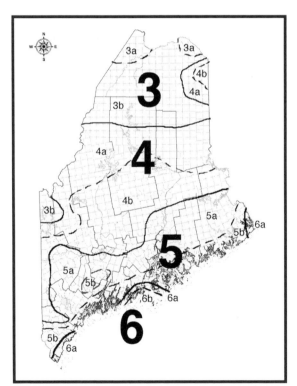

Figure 5.8. Plant Hardiness Zones for the state of Maine as developed by the USDA and available at www.usna. usda.gov.

atures below 24°F produce a severe freeze with very heavy damage to plants, particularly as the ground will often freeze solid depending on the duration and severity of the freeze, soil moisture, and soil type (Koss et al., 1988).

For the most part, the first freeze of the fall occurs 1 to 2 weeks after the first frost, so near the end of September in the north and early November along parts of the midcoast and in the Eastport region(Fig. 5.7). As with frost, microclimates can play a role in the occurrence of the first freeze. Much like the relationship between the first frost and first freeze of fall, the last freeze is about ten days earlier than the last frost statewide. And the same variability based upon location applies to the last freeze of spring as well, that is the last freeze will occur up to two months earlier in coastal and southern parts of the state.

The freeze-free period paints a slightly better picture than the growing season that's based on the first and last frosts. Freeze-free periods generally range between about 120 and 180 days across the state, that is, 4 to 6 months of the year. The immediate areas around Port Clyde and Eastport appear to average nearly 200 days without a killing freeze. Consequently, the growing season of many major crops adds variety to the garden, provided they are able to survive the first frost.

In addition to the interest in frost and freeze occurrence for vegetable growers, many gardeners are also interested in growing certain flowers. The yardstick for choosing flowers for a particular area is the plant hardiness zone of a species. The U. S. Department of Agriculture produces maps indicating these zones around the country. The boundaries of individual zones are based on the average minimum temperature for the winter. The major zones are based on 10°F increments, with a further division into sub-zones (a–b) based on 5°F increments. The great range of plant hardiness zones exemplifies Maine's great variety in climate. There are four zones (3–6) north to south across the state over a distance of only 300 miles (Fig. 5.8). This is an exceptional range when compared to the entire United States. It also illustrates the great winter climate gradient across the state.

Zone 3, with an average lowest winter temperature between -30 and -40°F, occupies the upper 1/4 to 1/3 of the state, with another small area tucked into the western mountains. Zone 4 (-20 – -30°F) occupies most of the central part of the state, basically from Bangor north and along most of the western border with New Hampshire. The major cities of the southern part of the state all fall into Zone 5 (-10 to -20°F), and the immediate coastal areas fall into Zone 6 (0 to -10°F). Again, small microclimatic conditions, such as proximity to a house or shelter underneath trees, can affect the hardiness of your plants. Plants in protected areas may be able to survive along the border of zones in which they would normally be unable to survive. On the other hand, it may be wise to choose plants that are hardy in a lower zone if you live close to the boundary of two hardiness zones. One or two winters with low temperatures that exceed the lower boundary of a zone could result in some plants not surviving the winter. This may hold especially true if there is a lack of snow cover. A decent snow pack will insulate plants and protect them from wind, allowing some to survive under temperatures that would usually be too severe.

■ TEMPERATURE EXTREMES

Tales of the hardiness of Mainers may stem from the number of temperature extremes during the year or from a major weather event from the past. Extreme variations in temperature can occur with both the cold of winter and the heat of summer, as Maine may have both in any given year. The northwestern third of the state will have a daily minimum temperature of 32°F or below more than 200 days, a whopping 55% of the year (Fig. 5.9). In fact, about half the state drops below freezing half the time during any one year (180 days). Even coastal areas drop below freezing 130–140 days during the year (about 35–38% of the time in any one year).

Perhaps the real measure of how Mainers are so adapted to the chilly climate of the state is the number of days that low temperatures drop below 0°F. There is something mystical about getting into negative numbers. Of course, the grinding of the car engine as it works to turn over is a sound all too familiar on sub-zero winter mornings. Nearly the entire northern two-thirds of the state will experience at least one month per year (30 days) when low temperatures fall below 0°F, although northernmost parts of the state, such as the Allagash region, experience twice that number (Fig. 5.9). Sub-zero temperatures are not that uncommon in the midcoast and the Eastport region, either, as these areas fall below zero up to 10 days per year.

Daily low temperature may be the parameter that epitomizes the harshness of Maine's winters, but daily high temperatures that remain below freezing are as much an icon of Maine's weather and climate. Moreover, daily highs that remain below freezing are key contributors to keeping lakes and ponds frozen for skating, hockey, and ice fishing. On average, northern parts of the state have more than 90 days a year that fail to get above freezing (Fig. 5.9). Most of the rest of the state has at least 50 days when the high temperature is below 32°F. As a result, most of the state will have at least two months during the year with sub-freezing temperatures. It is only Port Clyde and southernmost Maine that have fewer than 40 days with high temperatures below freezing.

Extremely frigid conditions, characterized by daily high temperatures that fail to break 0°F, occur at least once a year over most of the upper half of the state. Northernmost areas and parts of the western mountains average 3 or 4 days a year when temperatures fail to get above 0°F, and Van Buren averages more than 4 days a year of sub-zero high temperatures. You certainly have to keep an eye on your water pipes on those days. The southern half of the state will not usually reach this low mark in a given year. In these areas, maximum temperatures that remain below zero occur only once every three years. This is particularly evident as you near the coast.

Although not as dramatic as cold weather extremes, hot temperatures are, nevertheless, notable in Maine. One limit often used to identify excessive heat is a daily high temperature that breaks the 90°F mark. For instance, temperatures exceeding 90°F on three successive days constitutes a heat wave. That designation is purely arbitrary, however, as there is no scientific basis for using 90°F as the boundary for classifying a hot spell as a heat wave. Daily high temperatures exceeding 90°F occur most frequently in the south-central part of the state, particularly in the Lewiston and Augusta areas (Fig. 5.10). Those urban

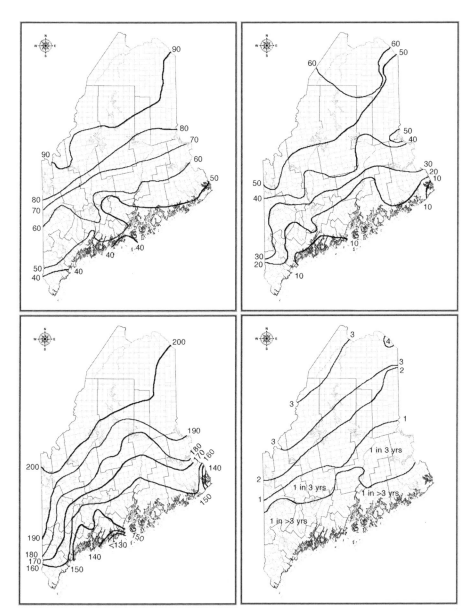

Figure 5.9. Average number of days per year by region with daily high temperature of less than 32°F (top left), daily low temperature of less than 0°F (top right), daily low temperature of less than 32°F (bottom left) and daily high temperature of less than 0°F (bottom right).

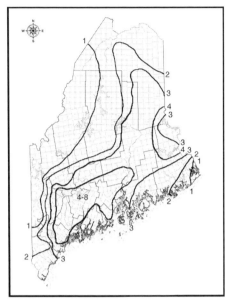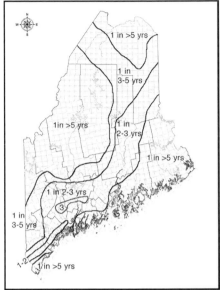

Figure 5.10. Average number of days per year by region with daily high temperature of greater than 90°F (left), and daily low temperature of greater than 70°F (right).

centers average eight days a year with high temperatures of at least 90°F. Areas surrounding these cities and extending eastward toward Bangor average closer to four days a year with such high temperatures. Most of the rest of the state averages from 1 to 4 days, with the exception being the hilly westernmost part of the state and around Eastport. These regions usually will not have high temperatures of at least 90°F in any given year. This may explain why Maine is such a magnet for tourists from more southern climates wishing to get away from the heat of summer.

There is no daily low commonly used to express an uncomfortable night of sleep, but if you had to pick a number, 70°F would be an ideal limit. On the rare occasions that summer nights fail to get below 70°F, you might wish for that air conditioner. Nighttime lows above 70°F occur every year, on average, in a very small section of the southern part of the state (Fig. 5.10). The hot spots of Lewiston and Augusta will have a daily minimum above 70°F maybe 3 times a year. A small swath from Sanford to Portland may have one or two nights with such warm temperatures. Most of the rest of the state will have no low temperatures above 70°F in a given year. In fact, in most parts of the state, it takes 2–5 years to have such a warm night during the summer. Much of the western mountain region and extreme northern Maine, together with Down East and Washington County will only have a nighttime low of 70°F or greater every five years or more—not exactly a concern for individuals in those parts of the state.

The yearly extremes are quite impressive, but even more impressive are the record high and low temperatures from around the state. Perhaps the most astounding fact is

Table 5.2. Record Low Temperature for Long-Term Climate Stations in Maine as of 2009.

Town	Temperature (°F)	Date with Comments
Big Black River	-50	16 January 2009 – Coldest temperature ever recorded Maine
Van Buren	-47	22 January 1984
Allagash	-45	26, 27 January 1994 – Part of January 1994 cold spell
Rangeley	-45	20 January 1994 – Part of January 1994 cold spell
Squa Pan Dam	-45	9 February 1934
Jackman	-44	2 February 1962 – One of coldest dates statewide
Bridgewater	-43	20 January 1994 – Part of January 1994 cold spell
Clayton Lake	-43	2 February 1962 – One of coldest dates statewide
Fort Kent	-42	14, 15 January 1957
Millinocket	-42	2 February 1962 – One of coldest dates statewide
Ripogenus Dam	-42	9 February 1934
Caribou	-41	1 February 1955
Houlton	-41	4 January 1981
Gardiner	-41	24 January 1907
Presque Isle	-41	19 January 1925
Woodland	-41	30 December 1933
Madison	-40	30 December 1933
Orono	-40	17 January 1907
Brassua Dam	-39	2, 3 February 1962 – One of coldest dates statewide
Corinna	-39	2 February 1962 – One of coldest dates statewide
Farmington	-39	20 January 1994 – Part of January 1994 cold spell
North Bridgton	-39	16 February 1943
Waterville	-39	30 December 1933
Danforth	-38	31 December 1989
Long Falls Dam	-37	1 January 1972, 2 February 1962
Eustis	-36	7, 8 February 1993
Rumford	-36	20 January 1994 – Part of January 1994 cold spell
Vanceboro	-35	19 January 1971
Middle Dam	-34	11 January 1976
Augusta	-33	19 January 1975
Ellsworth	-33	4 January 1981
Dover-Foxcroft	-31	20 January 1994 – Part of January 1994 cold spell
Bangor Airport	-30	2 February 1962 – One of coldest dates statewide
Brunswick	-30	4 January 1981
Lewiston	-28	19 January 1925
Sanford	-28	18 January 1957
Jonesboro	-26	31 December 1989
Portland	-26	19 January 1971
Bar Harbor	-25	7 January 1916
Eastport	-23	12 February 1914

Note: Not all record temperatures for the state shown here, and not all stations cover the same time period. Data based on files available from National Climatic Data Center. However, in some cases, there may have been temperatures that were lower for individual stations than given here, but the dates did not seem to agree with other temperatures from around the region, thus they were not listed here. An older site in Bangor recorded –32 on 10 February 1948 and an older site in Vanceboro recorded –39°F on 15 January 1905.

Table 5.3. Record High Temperature for Long-Term Climate Stations in Maine as of 2009.

Town	Temperature (°F)	Date with Comments
North Bridgton	105	4 July 1911 – Highest temperature ever recorded
Brunswick	104	2 August 1975 – "Hot Saturday"
Farmington	104	10 July 1911 – Part of severe July 1911 heat wave
Hiram	104	7 July 1939
Jonesboro	104	3 August 1975
Orono	104	18 August 1935
Squa Pan Dam	104	15 June 1930 – earliest 100+°F recorded during the year
Gardiner	103	2 August 1975 – "Hot Saturday"
Portland	103	2 August 1975 – "Hot Saturday"
Bangor Airport	102	2 August 1975 – "Hot Saturday"
Houlton	102	7 July 1911– Part of severe July 1911 heat wave
Jackman	102	5 July 1897
Lewiston	102	4 July 1911 – Part of severe July 1911 heat wave
Madison	102	11 July 1911– Part of severe July 1911 heat wave
Woodland	02	18 August 1935
Bar Harbor	101	2 August 1975 – "Hot Saturday"
Grand Lake Stream	101	3 August 1975
Millinocket	101	18 June 1907
Newcastle	101	2 August 1975 – "Hot Saturday"
Sanford	101	2 August 1975 – "Hot Saturday"
Waterville	101	1 August 1975 and 4 July 1911
Augusta	100	5 August 1955
Bridgton	100	3 Auguest 1975
Ellsworth	100	2 August 1975 – "Hot Saturday"
Rumford	100	2 August 1975 –"Hot Saturday"
Presque Isle	99	11 July 1911 – Part of severe July 1911 heat wave
Ripogenus Dam	99	19 August 1935
Belfast	98	19 July 1946
Eastport	98	18 July 1999
Fort Kent	98	29 June 1893
Vanceboro	98	2 August 1975 – "Hot Saturday"
Corinna	97	23 May 1977
Bridgewater	96	2 August 1975 – "Hot Saturday"
Caribou	96	22 May 1977
Danforth	96	26 June 1905
Middle Dam	96	3 August 1975
Allagash	95	16 June 2001
Van Buren	95	20 July 1991
Rangeley	94	10 September 2002

Note: Not all record temperatures for the state shown here, and not all stations cover the same time period. Data from files available from the National Climatic Data Center. However, in some cases, there may have been temperatures that were lower for individual stations than given here, but the dates did not seem to agree with other temperatures from around the region, thus they were not listed here. An older site in Bangor recorded 104°F on 16 July 1928 and an older site in Eustis recorded 104°F on 13 August 1944. An older site in Rumford recorded 101°F on 4 July 1911.

the difference between the lowest temperature ever recorded in the state (Table 5.2) and the highest temperature ever recorded (Table 5.3). The lowest temperature was −50°F on the Big Black River on January 16, 2009, and the highest temperature was 105°F in North Bridgton on July 4, 1911. The difference between the two, thus, the potential range of temperatures felt in the state is 152°F. You don't have to look any further to see the great variability in weather around the state. Interestingly, there are at least 16 climate stations around the state whose record low temperatures are −40°F or less and another 16 stations whose record lows are at least −30°F (Table 5.3). On the opposite end of the temperature spectrum, there are at least 24 additional stations whose record high temperatures are at least 100°F. This includes two 100°+F readings for Bangor, one from the present station at the airport and one from the pre-1953 station. Quite impressive numbers, considering that of all the temperature data discussed here, the cold stands out as the prime characteristic of the Maine's weather.

■ THE JANUARY THAW

Most Mainers are well aware of that time in mid-January when temperatures warm, sometimes high enough to start melting existing snow. This is the January thaw and many people enjoy this brief period of warmer temperatures before the last frigid conditions at the end of the month and into February. After all, there are some places around the state where the coldest day of the year occurs in early February. The January thaw is a climatic singularity, meaning that it occurs just about every year. There are some winters when the thaw does not occur, but it is, on average, a distinct event that shows up in climatic records.

The next question about the January thaw then becomes when. An additional question may be, what temperature value best defines the thaw? Records indicate the thaw occurs during the third week in January. This is the warmest time of the month, with temperatures falling again until mid-February, when temperatures begin their steady rise to the warmth of spring and summer. It is fairly easy to define the thaw because all three temperature re-cords (maximum, mean, minimum) peak fairly consistently around the 24th–26th.

The cause for the January thaw, not only in Maine, but also throughout New England, is not completely understood. It appears that the Bermuda High has a tendency to move a bit farther west and north during mid-January, allowing warmer air to move into the northeast. It is unclear why that pressure system may shift position at this particular time in January. Some scientists feel the January thaw may not exist at all when tested for statisti-cally; the eye, however, is often a better judge than the numbers. The January thaw is clearly part of Maine's winter climate, that short but sweet reprieve from the bitter cold.

6

PRECIPITATION

The aspect of the weather that sparks the greatest day-to-day anxiety, particularly as you prepare for an upcoming event, is precipitation. The availability of long-range forecasts may give you an early idea of what will happen precipitation-wise, but the uncertainty of these forecasts just adds to the anxiety. This chapter discusses the causes of precipitation in Maine, how it is distributed throughout the year by seasons and months, and how it is distributed across the state.

I'll discuss precipitation here as total precipitation, meaning that snowfall amounts are converted to their liquid water equivalent. The most commonly used conversion is that ten inches of snow is equivalent to one inch of water; however this conversion can be quite different from one snowfall to the next. For instance, with a very wet snow, it may only take four or five inches of snow to equal one inch of water, and a very dry fluffy snow may require up to 14 or 15 inches of snow to equal an inch of water. The latter is more rare in Maine than the former. Specifics on solid precipitation like snow and ice are discussed in Chapter 7.

■ WHAT CONTROLS MAINE'S PRECIPITATION?

Precipitation forms when rising air cools to the point that water vapor condenses into liquid droplets. These droplets grow in size and number, forming clouds. The droplets continue to grow until they are heavy enough to overcome gravity and fall to the ground as liquid precipitation (rain) provided temperatures remain above freezing during much of the droplets' final descent. Liquid droplets that evaporate before they reach the ground are called virga. Given that the process of precipitation begins with rising air, there are several processes that produce precipitation in Maine.

The first process has two possible components: a low-pressure system (a storm) moving through the state or passing close by, or any frontal systems associated with a low-pressure system sliding across the state, even though the low-pressure system itself may be situated well north of Maine. Regardless of whether or not the low-pressure system or the associated fronts pass across the state, each component has the potential to cause precipitation. The presence of low-pressure systems affecting the state are most common in the fall, winter, and spring when temperature contrasts are the greatest. The major storm tracks, particularly the coastal track (Fig. 3.6), are more active during these times of the year. During the summer, the most active storm track usually moves the low-pressure systems north of Maine, but the trailing fronts may still cause precipitation across the state. Furthermore, tropical

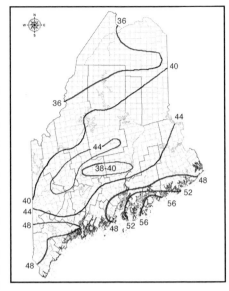

Figure 6.1. Mean annual precipitation across the state of Maine. Contour lines interpolated between existing climatic stations.

systems, including hurricanes, can produce large rain events during the late summer and early fall.

The second major cause of precipitation around the state is more prevalent during the summer months. With daytime heating of the land, the air above the ground is warmed, causing it to rise. This is called convection, and it results in the occurrence of afternoon showers. The process is enhanced when the air mass over the state is very warm and humid, as this adds instability to the air column and increases the likelihood that rising air will produce showers. During the early parts of the day, the rising air will produce fluffy, mashed-potato-like cumulus clouds. With continued heating of the land throughout the day, more and more air rises and the cumulus clouds grow vertically, eventually reaching the point that precipitation occurs. Unlike precipitation associated with a low-pressure system that may cover the entire state or large areas of it, convective showers are more scattered. This leads to the common summer forecast of scattered afternoon showers or thundershowers. Thunderstorms result when the process of rising air is vigorous enough to produce very tall clouds (cumulonimbus clouds or thunderheads) and the separation of electrical charges that results in the formation of lightning.

Regardless of which scenario is active, the mountains of western Maine enhance the rising of air. This is why precipitation amounts may be higher in those parts of the state for any given storm and why afternoon showers are more prevalent there. In fact, any time there is unstable air over the state as a whole, the mountains make the formation of precipitation more likely.

Figure 6.2. Photograph from Lower Togue Pond of Mt. Katahdin, highest point in Maine, and possibly the wettest point in the state given its elevation. Photograph by Catie Zielinski.

Much like the impact mountains have on precipitation, the ocean also has a significant effect on precipitation in the state. The Gulf of Maine and the Atlantic Ocean provide a readily available source of moisture that can produce very high precipitation amounts from some storms. This may be especially true for coastal parts of the state. In addition, the ocean can provide a source of moisture even when a high-pressure system may be exerting a great amount of influence on our weather. When a high-pressure system is located east to northeast of Maine, the airflow will be from the east or an onshore flow. Despite the fact that a high-pressure system dominates our weather, this easterly flow can bring moisture in off the ocean, producing light rain or drizzle, especially Down East. Usually when this occurs, precipitation amounts will not be very great.

■ PRECIPITATION DISTRIBUTION

Mean (average) annual precipitation (MAP) values vary from the mid-30s to the mid-50s (in inches) as you move from the extreme northwestern part of the state to the Acadia and Down East coastal regions (Fig. 6.1). Over the entire record for the state (1895–2007), the statewide average MAP is 42.64 inches. The spatial distribution is quite easy to explain given the controls on precipitation. With the Gulf of Maine right on the doorstep, it is no wonder that the highest average precipitation totals are found along the coast. It is very likely that the higher mountains, such as Katahdin (5,267 ft. Fig. 6.2), Sugarloaf (4,250 ft), and the Bigelows (4,145 ft.), receive more precipitation, but there are no high-altitude weather

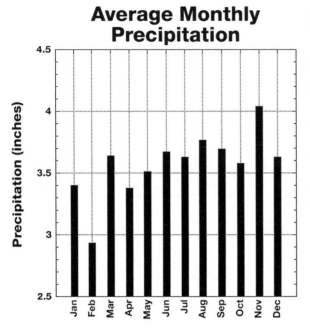

Average Monthly Precipitation

Figure 6.3. Mean monthly precipitation for the state of Maine.

stations to measure it. For instance, Mt. Washington (6,288 ft.) in New Hampshire receives almost 99 inches of precipitation per year, so it is likely that some Maine mountains could easily receive 80–90 inches of annual precipitation. As the wettest part of the state is closest to the ocean, the driest part is the area farthest from this large moisture source. Essentially the northwestern third of the state receives less than 40 inches of precipitation per year, with the areas north of the higher mountains (the Allagash region) receiving less than 36 inches per year. The western and central hills probably exert a bit of a rain shadow effect on the northwestern part of the state as the hills may prevent some of the precipitation originating in coastal storm systems from reaching the Allagash region. Interestingly, a second relatively dry part of the state is the central region extending from Bangor westward toward Madison and Skowhegan. The cause of this may perhaps be the nature of the storm tracks that affect Maine (Fig. 3.6). One major track is up the coast while another moves down the St. Lawrence River Valley. It may be that this portion of Maine is situated between these two tracks, reducing the overall amount of precipitation just enough to show up on statewide measurements. The remainder of the MAP pattern across the state falls into the trend of increasing precipitation amounts as you head toward the coast.

The distribution of average statewide precipitation by month shows an interesting pattern (Fig. 6.3); but the fascinating aspect of the pattern is, in fact, the lack of a distinct seasonal precipitation pattern. Unlike so many other parts of the United States, Maine does not have a wet or dry season. For instance, most of the United States east of the Rocky Mountains receives the bulk of their precipitation during the summer primarily from afternoon showers and thunderstorms. The two exceptions to this are the Great Lakes region, which receives a bulk of its annual precipitation via lake-effect snows, and eastern New England, particularly Down East areas. Easternmost Maine receives more precipitation during the winter.

November is the wettest month for Maine, averaging 3.98 inches; but this is only one inch more than February, the driest month, with an average of 2.97 inches. Although

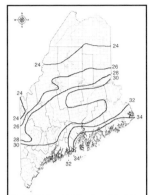

Figure 6.4. Number of days per year where the amount of precipitation equals or exceeds 0.1 inch (left), 0.5 inch (center), and 1.0 inch (right).

there is not much difference between them, there is a plausible explanation for the trend. The coastal storm track starts to become dominant in November, so Maine is more susceptible to its potentially greater precipitation. In addition, the contrast between land and ocean temperatures gets higher, which helps fuel storm development. The lower precipitation in February may be a function of the position of the strong high-pressure systems that migrate across Canada during the winter months. In February, this high is often located around Hudson Bay (Ludlum, 1976) and given this position, it will often keep Maine under a pattern of fair weather with a dry northwest airflow.

The November maximum and February minimum effect seasonal precipitation. An average of 11.17 inches makes fall the wettest season. Winter is the driest, at 9.99 inches. Summer across the state averages 11.01 inches and spring averages 10.46 inches. Nevertheless, the seasonal differences are only on the order of one inch from maximum to minimum, not a great difference from a climatological perspective given that the MAP for Maine is more than 42 inches.

Although there is no distinct wet season, there is a notable seasonal distribution from a regional perspective. The northern and western parts of Aroostook County exhibit an increase in summer precipitation, with July and August being the wettest months of the year in areas like Caribou. However, as you move south and east toward the foothills and coastal regions, precipitation amounts are more equally distributed throughout the year, with a slight maximum in November. The primary cause for the summer maximum in the more northern and interior parts may be the greater frequency of summer showers in those areas compared to parts of the state more likely to feel the effects of the ocean water. The cool sea breeze that becomes prevalent during the summer stabilizes the air and inhibits the convection that leads to summer showers. Interior sections are more susceptible to daytime heating, rising air, and afternoon showers and thundershowers. Frequent winter storms associated with the Atlantic track add to greater precipitation being received during the winter in coastal and near-coastal parts of the state.

■ PRECIPITATION EXTREMES

The differences between coastal and inland precipitation can be seen in the average number of days with precipitation of a given amount. Maine usually has between about 80 and 100 days during the year when at least a tenth of an inch of precipitation falls (Fig. 6.4). The north-central part of the state has the greatest number of days with precipitation—90–100—probably reflecting the more frequent occurrence of summer showers. The lower end of the range—slightly less than 80 to 85—is found in the southern and coastal areas. The lower numbers undoubtedly reflect fewer summer showers. On the other hand, when looking at larger precipitation amounts, such as a half to one inch per day, coastal areas, particularly in the Acadia region, have more days with these higher amounts (Fig. 6.4). Northern Maine receives about 24 days per year with more than a half inch and only 4–6 days with more than one inch of precipitation, whereas coastal and Down East areas receive 32–34 days with more than a half inch and 12–16 days with more than an inch of precipitation (Fig. 6.4). The greater frequency of large precipitation events toward the coast reflects the proximity of the Gulf of Maine and the greater influence of coastal storms.

■ THE WET AND THE DRY

Although Maine is generally thought of as a wet state—at times the amount of precipitation can be overwhelming—there are some years or periods of years when precipitation amounts are not sufficient to keep ground-water systems at adequate levels, causing vegetation to wilt and die. When this happens, drought conditions may be reached. Drought is a complex climatological event. The amount of rain in one case may cause drought conditions to exist, but at another time that same amount will not lead to drought; and there are several types of drought. The time of year the precipitation falls plays an important part. During the summer, warmer temperatures will cause more of the rain that falls to evaporate and vegetation will take up much more water than would happen during a cooler time of year. In other words, precipitation is much more effective during the cooler time of year. It is important to get adequate precipitation to help replenish water supplies during the spring after the snowmelt and before trees leaf out. At this time, most precipitation that falls will go toward replenishing water systems.

This leads to the variety in the types of drought. A meteorological drought occurs simply when there is not enough precipitation. At one time, the National Weather Service considered meteorological drought conditions to be in existence when 75% or less of the average precipitation has fallen. Very often under these conditions the precipitation amounts will not equal the combined loss of water to the atmosphere as vapor from evaporation and from transpiration by plants (evapotranspiration). A second type of drought is a hydrological drought. In this case, both surface- and ground-water levels have dropped to the point where they are not adequate to support water supply systems for humans and vegetation. A hydrological drought is produced by meteorological drought conditions, but the timing of the hydrological drought lags behind the meteorological drought. It may take only a brief period of time for water levels to reach the critical stage following low precipitation amounts, yet water levels may remain critical even once precipitation amounts begin to increase again. Although the meteorological drought may end, the slow movement of water into the ground, and especially into the ground-water systems, will keep water levels under hydrologically adequate conditions for a longer period of time. This was the case in early 2002 following the severe drought of 2001. Spring snow and rain produced enough precipitation for many backyards to be saturated during the spring, yet there was still talk of drought conditions, because ground-water levels were still way down from the severe drought of the previous year. The third type of drought is an agricultural drought. In this case, precipitation amounts are low enough that vegetation wilts. This can happen very quickly, even when a true meteorological drought does not occur. An agricultural drought can be a seasonal phenomenon or it could simply be a function of vegetation type.

7

SNOW AND ICE

Although snow and ice are solid forms of precipitation, they play such an integral part in Maine's weather that they deserve to be talked about on their own. Depending on where you are in the state, winter-like precipitation may fall anytime from September to May, a mind-boggling nine months out of the year. Average conditions are not that extreme, as some parts of the state are more likely only to see snow between October and April—a time period that is still more than half the year. The words snow, sleet, and freezing rain can bring chills to even the most seasoned traveler in Maine, as roads may become virtual skating rinks.

■ WHAT CONTROLS MAINE'S SNOWFALL

There are two types of storm systems responsible for most of the snow we see in Maine. The most notorious are those that follow the Atlantic track up the eastern seaboard (see Fig. 3.6). These coastal storms, or nor'easters, named for the northeast winds off the ocean that characterize them, are responsible for the highest snowfalls throughout the state. A nor'easter typically forms in one of two ways, first as a single low-pressure system that forms in the western part of the Gulf of Mexico, close to Texas. These storms usually move eastward across the Gulf of Mexico, turning northward along the East Coast. Very often they seem to jump from Florida or Georgia to a point around Cape Hatteras, North Carolina, and in the process they often intensify. From there they progress up the coast, either moving out to sea before reaching Maine or moving along the Maine coastline and into the Canadian Maritimes. The second common way involves the development of a secondary storm. In this scenario, the initial storm will often move into the Northeast via the Ohio River Valley or across the Great Lakes. This storm will begin to weaken or "fill-in." Then a secondary low-pressure system will begin to form somewhere off the mid-Atlantic coastline or possibly toward the Gulf of Maine. The first storm will transfer its energy to this second storm, which then becomes the primary coastal storm.

Regardless of the method of development, a frequent characteristic of a nor'easter is that it often intensifies or deepens very quickly. A storm whose central low-pressure drops 24 mb over 24 hours is referred to as a meteorological bomb. This rapid deepening will produce very strong winds and very intense snowfall rates—both often a part of major nor'easters. At times these very strong storms appear to have an eye, much like a hurricane (Fig. 7.1).

Of course, not all nor'easters are strictly heavy snow producers as that depends on the all-important storm track. The easiest way to predict whether you will get all snow, a mixture of everything (snow, sleet, freezing rain, rain), or just rain is to determine what side of the storm you will be on. If the storm moves to your west, you will be on the warm east side and precipitation will likely be all rain. If the storm moves east of you, then you will be on the cold west side and you may very well get all snow. If the storm moves over you, then you could easily get all types of precipitation. These are only generalizations, but here are some common scenarios:

Scenario 1: The storm is well off the coast of Maine. In this situation, western Maine and especially the west side of the mountains may get very little snow. Interior sections and the eastern slopes of the hills may get a little more snow, but the heaviest snows will be along the coast, especially in Down East sections. This would probably be an all-snow event for areas that received any precipitation.

Scenario 2: The storm is slightly off the coast of Maine. In this situation, western parts of the state and the mountains may get moderate amounts of snow with higher amounts along the eastern slopes of the hills. Interior sections may get the heaviest snow from this scenario. Coastal areas may start as snow, but then precipitation very well may change to mixed precipitation and possibly rain as warmer air is brought into midlevels of the atmosphere off the ocean. This changes the snow to mixed precipitation. However, the warmer air may penetrate farther inland than expected for a given track if the storm is very intense. Warmer air can often move up the Penobscot River, turning the snow to mixed precipitation even past Bangor.

Scenario 3: The storm moves up along the coastline. Moderate to heavy snows may blanket western Maine, especially in the mountains. Interior sections may start as snow, but would then likely change to mixed precipitation and potentially rain. Coastal areas may start as snow, but the precipitation would quickly change to mixed precipitation and very likely to all rain.

Scenario 4: The storm moves inland, but stays on the east side of the mountains. In this situation, western Maine may get mostly snow, although the pos-

Figure 7.1. Satellite image of a large nor'easter that hit the state of Maine in January of 2002. The low-pressure in the center of the storm produces an eye much like that produced by a hurricane. This particular storm was exceptionally intense, with a central low-pressure of 956 mb at its peak intensity. The storm produced more than 2 feet of snow in parts of the state and the very strong north winds pushed the tide out in Portland, resulting in a much lower tidal level than predicted. Note the difference in the effect of strong winds on tidal levels as compared to the Groundhog Day storm in Chapter 13. Image courtesy of Hendricus Lulofs, Caribou NWS.

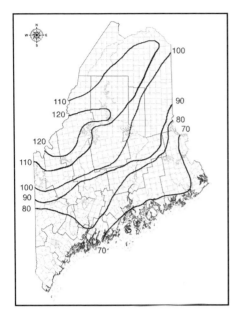
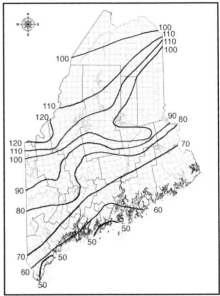

Figure 7.2. Average long-term snowfall amounts (left) and average snowfall amounts from the early 1970s to early 2000s (right). Right figure was produced by the Caribou NWS office and formerly was available on the Web site at www.erh.noaa.gov/er/car.

sibility exists of a changeover to mixed precipitation. The same situation may hold true for the mountains, though higher elevations may receive all snow, which is good news for ski areas. Interior sections may start as snow, but precipitation would likely convert to mixed precipitation with the likelihood that most of the event would be rain. Coastal areas would probably just get rain in this situation.

Scenario 5: The storm moves up the west side of the Appalachians eventually moving down the St. Lawrence River Valley. This is the worst scenario of all for snow lovers. The only part of the state that may get any snow out of this track is the mountains, and maybe a very brief period of snow in westernmost Maine. However, any precipitation that starts as snow would probably quickly change to mixed precipitation and then rain. Interior sections and coastal areas would likely get all rain out of this track.

Regardless of the track taken, once the storm passes north to northeast of Maine, there is often a period of instability in the atmosphere, with very strong and cold northwest winds. It is possible that northern areas could easily get another inch or two the day after the major event from snow showers and snow squalls generated by this instability. Northernmost Maine can pick up several inches or more after the primary storm has moved into the Maritimes.

The second major type of storm that brings snow to Maine is the Alberta Clipper (Fig. 3.6). This system typically forms around Alberta, Canada, from where it often dips into the northern part of the United States. It then moves quickly through the Great Lakes and into New England. Since these are fast-moving storms, they usually drop no more than 8 inches of snow and that is usually in the area close to the track of the central low-pressure system. Snowfall totals often drop off quickly away from the center of the storm. There are times, however, when an Alberta Clipper will explode once it reaches the Gulf of Maine. When that happens, the storm can be very intense, essentially becoming a nor'easter and bringing heavy snows and strong winds to parts of Maine. Down East sections of the state can get clobbered when a storm like this forms.

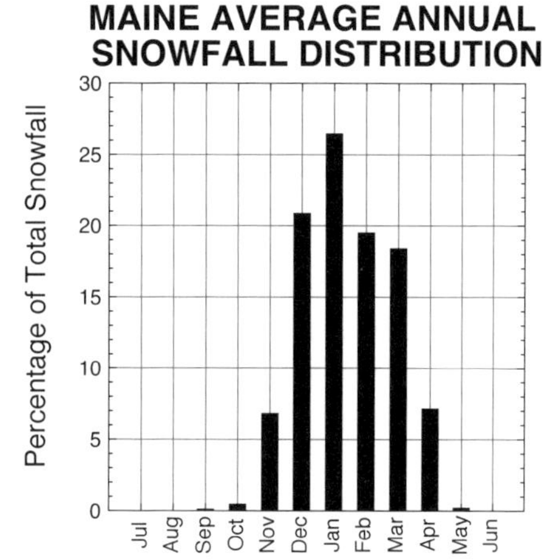

MAINE AVERAGE ANNUAL SNOWFALL DISTRIBUTION

Figure 7.3. Monthly average snowfall for Maine.

There are occasions where atmospheric conditions bring a strong flow of air off the ocean and significant snowfall along the coast. This is the NORLUN situation (discussed at the beginning). A NORLUN often forms when there is a strong storm offshore; the shape of the Maine coastline plays a role in focusing the snow belts. This situation can produce snowfall rates of 3–4 inches per hour, bringing things to a standstill. Mariners may be especially susceptible to the impact of a NORLUN given the poor visibility from strong winds and heavy snow. Coastal parts of Maine can also receive ocean-effect snows, much like the lake-effect snows that hit areas east of the Great Lakes, such as Buffalo. However, the airflow off of the water that produces ocean-effect snows rarely attains the intensity and persistence that produces the mind-boggling snowfalls in areas around the Great Lakes. Most ocean-effect situations drop only a few inches of snow over an extended period of time. Ocean-effect snow forms when very cold air moves over the open water, producing significant evaporation of ocean water. The vapor will condense and precipitation occurs as the air moves over land and encounters greater friction from the surface.

■ SNOWFALL DISTRIBUTION

The dominant northwest to southeast variations in weather patterns and climatic parameters is once again prevalent in snowfall patterns. The long-term pattern of snowfall amounts ranges from more than 120 inches/year in the valley portions of the western mountains to between 60 and 70 inches in the midcoast to Down East parts of the state (Fig. 7.2). The mountains themselves undoubtedly receive much more snow than 120 inches/year, but because there are no high-altitude climate stations in Maine, it's impossible to know for sure. The greater snow accumulation in more northern regions is more a function of overall temperature distribution than proximity to the ocean and dominant storm track. In fact, proximity to the ocean is often a cause for lower snowfall amounts in a coastal storm (as described above). The intrusion of colder air into the northern parts of the state during many winter precipitation events produces snow when southern or coastal areas receive rain.

By presenting long-term averages, we can take some of the variability out of yearly snowfall amounts because of the cyclical nature of Maine's snowfall. As discussed in Chapter 3, the decadal variability of the North Atlantic Oscillation (NAO) appears to be a prevalent control on overall snowfall amounts. For instance, average snowfall over the last 30 years shows lower overall totals, particularly in the south-central and coastal parts of the state (Fig. 7.2). Some areas along the coast have only been averaging 50 inches a year over the last 30 years, almost 30 inches less than the long-term average. A positive NAO, mode, meaning more low-snow years, particularly during the 1980s and 90s, dominated the last 30 years.

The snowiest month statewide is January, with an average of 27 inches (Fig. 7.3). December is the second snowiest, averaging 21 inches, followed by February's 19 inches. March is just a bit lower than February, but then November and April average only about 7 to 8 inches and most of that snow falls in the central interior and northern parts of the state. Likewise, the less than 1 inch that occurs during October and May is primarily restricted to northern parts of the state. Only a few tenths of an inch of snow falls in the state during September and that is usually in the north. However, some very big snow-storms can occur in early spring because of the great contrast in air masses, as warm, humid air from subtropical parts of the Atlantic Ocean begins to encroach into the cold, dry winter air still residing over much of the United States. This can set the stage for some major winter storms in late April and even early May.

■ TIMING OF SNOWFALL

As winter approaches there is often much anticipation for that first snow of the year. The first measurable snowfall of the year—at least 1/10 inch—occurs usually during the last week of October over most of the upper third of the state. Coastal sections receive their first measurable snow about a month later than The County, that is, the last week in November, or just in time for a "White Thanksgiving." The first snow of at least 1 inch comes about a week later, with the northwestern-most part of the state receiving its first inch or greater snow the first week of November and coastal parts of the state receiving their first inch or more the first week of December.

As anticipated as the first snowfall of the year may be, the last snow of the year is often downright annoying as your thoughts turn to spring. It can be especially disheart-ening once the crocuses have popped up. For the most part, both the last 1-inch or greater snowfall and the last measurable snowfall occur in April, except for the southwestern-most corner of the state. That part of the state, including the towns of Sanford and Ken-nebunkport, receives its last snow the last week of March. The overall distribution of

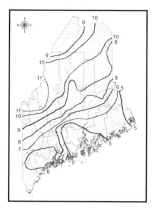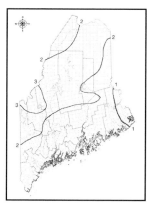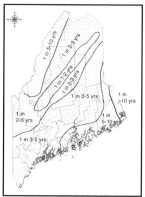

Figure 7.4. Average number of events per year by region with snowfall of 5 inches or more (left), 10 inches or more (center), and the average number of years between events of 18 inches or more (right).

the last 1-inch or greater snow is fairly regular across the state, but the last measurable snowfall distribution is very sporadic. This is not surprising as some late-season storms may have a small burst of snow at the end as colder air infiltrates into the state behind a cold front. This can produce a dusting of snow in many places. The last inch or greater snow will usually fall the first two weeks of April. The exception is the western mountains and northern parts of The County. Those areas receive their last inch or more of snow the third week of April.

■ SNOWFALL FREQUENCY

Now that we know when to expect the first snow, perhaps you're wondering how often Maine has a snowfall event of a given magnitude. Maine averages 28–48 days per year with at least 0.1 inch of snow. The greatest number of days of measurable snow occurs in a swath across the north-central part of the state. This part of the state has 40–48 days per year with measurable snow. The number of days with more than 0.1 inch of snow falls off from this area both north and toward the coast. The lowest number of days is found in the southwestern-most part of the state and the areas around Acadia and Eastport. The average number of days with at least 1 inch vary from 18–20 along the coast to just over one month (32 days) in the western mountains. The overall distribution across the state of the number of days with at least 1 inch of snow follows the northwest to southeast pattern of change.

Many people are probably more interested in the "big ones," those storms that make for great skiing, and of course, days off from school for the kids. The number of times per year that at least 5 inches of snow falls varies from 5–6 along the coast to 10–11 in the north (Fig. 7.4). Because snowfall amounts of that magnitude may fall over more than one 24-hour period, it makes more sense to look at them from an event point of view instead of by the number of days with that much snow. The difference between the two regions for 5-inch snows is not as great as you may expect, most likely because the heavy snows associated with coastal storms do not have as great an effect farther inland. In the case of 10-inch or greater snowfalls, much of the southern to central parts of the state receive one such event per year. Most of the rest of the state has two events per year of that magnitude, with a small section in the western mountains averaging three per year. Easternmost Washington County has a 10-inch snow or greater only every other year on average. No doubt the warming of air off the ocean helps to keep large snowfall amounts down in many coastal sites.

As for the "whopper" storms, those that dump 18 or more inches, on average, there is no occurrence of an event of that magnitude in a given year for the entire state. Areas within the center of the state may get such a big storm every 2 or 3 years, but most of the state will only get that much snow in one event once every 3–5 years. In fact, northwestern-most Maine, particularly those areas north of the mountains, can often be farther removed from some of the larger coastal storms. This produces snows of 18 inches or greater at the same rate (once every 5–10 years) as parts of the midcoast and Down East. Areas around Eastport and along the eastern part of Washington County rarely receive a snowfall event of 18 or more inches. Many of the larger storms often turn to rain in those parts of the state.

■ WHITE CHRISTMAS

One of the biggest questions in early and mid-December, and even as early as late November around Thanksgiving, is will there be a white Christmas. Snow on the ground during the holiday shopping season seems to add something to the experience; it puts you in the mood, so to speak. Certainly, living in Maine gives almost everyone in the state better than a 50-50 chance of having a white Christmas. A white Christmas, as defined by the National Weather Service, is at least one inch of snow on the ground sometime during the 24-hour period. In other words, it could start snowing late at night and technically still could qualify as a white Christmas. The other aspect of a white Christmas is that it does not have to be snowing on Christmas Day to qualify, although some purists may argue that point.

An evaluation back in 1995 by individuals at the National Climatic Data Center using average snow-depth readings from 1961 to

Table 7.1. Probability of a White Christmas for Several Sites in Maine Based on Snow-Depth records 1961-90.

Station	1 inch	5 inches	10 inches
Augusta	90%	2%	21%
Brunswick	80%	40%	17%
Caribou	97%	77%	57%
Houlton	96%	74%	52%
Portland	83%	43%	13%

Note: Data from Ross et al. (1995, NCDC Technical Report 95-03, p. 3). Percentages would probably be lower for the period 1971-2000

1990 gives an idea of the probability of having a white Christmas in a given year. These percentages probably would be a bit lower under the 1971–2000 norm now in use as the 1960s were rather snowy and the 1990s were generally less snowy. Nevertheless, the odds are still in favor of having a white Christmas almost anywhere in the state, with the greatest probability in the north and western mountains, and the lowest probability along the coast, as you would expect. Table 7.1 shows the probability of a white Christmas for several sites in Maine that had at least a 25-year continuous record from 1961 to 1990. The table also shows the likelihood of having enough snow (either 5 or 10 inches on the ground) to build a snowman on Christmas Day.

■ ICE STORMS

One of the worst situations during the winter occurs with ice storms. They may be worse than blizzards as far as their potential impact. Even thin icing, such as freezing rain or glaze, may be dangerous for travel and walking. While four-wheel-drive vehicles are able to get around in snow, they provide very little additional safety when an ice storm hits.

Ice storms are large freezing rain events, meaning there is significant accumulation of ice on all surfaces, resulting in downed trees, limbs, and wires. Often accumulations of more than a quarter inch will constitute an ice storm. Freezing rain is rain that freezes upon contact with a surface, meaning it forms a glaze on all surfaces (Fig. 7.5). The

Figure 7.5. Although ice storms can be very problematic, they make for beautiful scenery when the sun comes out. Here, ice has formed a heavy glaze on cedar trees after a period of freezing rain. Photo by Greg Zielinski.

process that forms freezing rain is a bit different than the cause of sleet. Sleet is ice pellets that reach the ground in their frozen form. The formation of sleet instead of freezing rain is a function of temperature conditions at and above the surface. During the winter, most precipitation begins to fall as snow. However, if warm air above freezing (32°F) has moved into the area at midlevels of the atmosphere, the snow will melt and turn to rain. Sleet or freezing rain forms if there is another freezing layer of air at the earth's surface. If that cold layer is thick enough, the rain re-freezes and falls as ice pellets or sleet. When the freezing layer is thin, the rain becomes super-cooled, but is unable to crystallize into ice. When super cooled

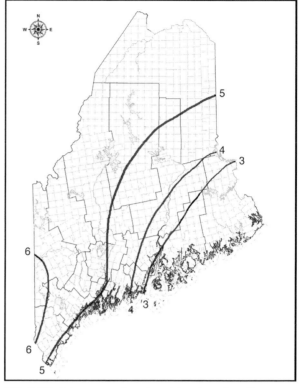

Figure 7.6. Average annual number of days by region with significant ice accumulation (.5 inch or more) from freezing rain.

rain hits the ground, it crystallizes, forming a glaze on surfaces (Fig. 7.5). Ther- are several ways for warm air to penetrate into the mid-layers of the atmosphere, and one of those occurs with almost all nor'easters: the flow of warm air off warm ocean waters. Icing events happen quite frequently in a given year, as can major ice storms. Most parts of the state will have between three and six days with significant ice accumulation, with higher numbers farther inland to both the north and west, and lower numbers near the coast (Fig. 7.6). Although many storms produce icing close to the coast, the frequent changeover to rain usually limits significant ice accumulation. On the other hand, the inland valleys are spots where cold air can pool, as it is denser than warm air. This is an ideal situation for major ice accumulation. Much of the precipitation may fall as freezing rain when warm air overrides the cold air that tends to linger in the valley.

8

HUMIDITY

Imagine a hot summer day, sitting in the shade, yet the sweat still rolls down your face. This may be the most common thought that comes to mind when you hear the word humidity. On the other hand, brushing along the carpet during the winter may give you a "shock" as you touch any piece of metal, someone else, or, especially, the cat. These are just two examples of how humidity is felt at any given time. Although Maine is often thought of as being a "wet" state, humidity levels can change quite drastically from day to day and especially from season to season.

Humidity is a reflection of the amount of water vapor in the air and subsequently how you react to the actual air temperature. The more water vapor there is in the air, the higher the humidity will be and the hotter the actual temperature will feel. The ultimate impact of humidity is the combination of high humidity together with high air temperatures that occurs during the dog days of summer. The evaporation of sweat is the way the body tries to cool itself, but on those days the high humidity prevents the sweat from evaporating off your skin. The sweat can build up on your skin and the body is unable to cool itself efficiently, even though you might be sitting in the shade. There is a method to determine how much the combination of high humidity and high air temperatures will impact people. The number derived by this combination is the Heat Index (Table 2.1). It reflects the potential danger to people, especially to the elderly. High humidity can easily raise the heat index to levels as much as 10°F higher than the actual air temperature. At the same time, high heat index levels can result in poor air quality, also producing unsafe conditions for those with respiratory problems.

The combination of high heat and humidity is almost always caused by a strong high-pressure system located south of Maine. This is a classic example of the impact of the Bermuda High, so-named because this high-pressure system often sits close to the is-

AVERAGE DEW POINT VS RELATIVE HUMIDITY

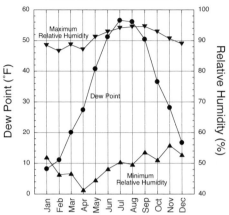

Figure 8.1. Average monthly relative humidity (maximum and minimum) and dew point across the state of Maine.

land of Bermuda. This allows very warm, humid air from the Gulf of Mexico or the subtropical Atlantic Ocean to flow into the state. When this high-pressure system is strong enough that it stops all weather systems from moving it out of the way, a situation referred to as a blocking high, the heat and humidity may persist for several days. For all practical purposes, a Bermuda high acts as a "heat pump," pushing warm humid air into the state. Relief is not often felt until another high-pressure system behind a cold front is large and strong enough to push the Bermuda high south of Maine.

In addition to high humidity combined with heat, think about those cool, bone-chilling days in fall and especially early winter when temperatures are low but the humidity is high. The cold seems to go right through to your bones. High humidity can affect the air temperature in two ways—in this case making it feel colder than it actually is. This situation can also occur during the summer, particularly along the coast as fog moves in. Fog is the ultimate product of high humidity and is discussed in greater detail in Chapter 9.

■ HUMIDITY NUMBERS

There are two primary methods commonly used by researchers and forecasters to describe or measure the amount of water vapor in the air: relative humidity and dew point. Relative humidity is the term most presented by weather forecasters, particularly on television and radio. Relative humidity is the amount of water vapor the air is capable of holding and is expressed as a percentage. When the air is saturated, as when it is raining, the relative humidity is at or near 100%. The lower the relative humidity, the drier the air. The method used to calculate relative humidity, however, is a function of air temperature. The higher the temperature, the more water vapor a given volume of air can hold (Fig. 8.1). The reverse is true for cold air; the lower the temperature, the less water vapor that can be held. Unfortunately, this is why the term is *relative* humidity; it can change drastically during the day as the temperature changes. During the warmth of midday, even with no change in the amount of water vapor in the air, the relative humidity decreases. At night, as the air cools, it is unable to hold the same amount of water vapor and relative humidity increases. This leads to the presence of dew on certain mornings or, if the temperature is below freezing, the presence of frost.

So relative humidity may not be the best way to describe how humid the air is and how it feels. Dew point is a much better method to describe overall humidity since dew point does not change with temperature fluctuations as long as there is no change in air mass over the state. Dew point is the temperature at which water vapor condenses. When air temperatures reach the dew point, dew or frost will form. Very windy conditions will prevent dew or frost from forming because it mixes the air and does not allow moisture droplets to settle onto surfaces. Calm conditions are ideal for the formation of dew and frost. The air temperature will not fall below the dew point, so it is a good indicator of how cold it may get at night, provided a new air mass is not moving into the state. If the temperature is nearly at the dew point by the time you go to bed, there is a very good chance there will be dew or frost the next morning. This is good to know in early spring or late fall as you try to protect your gardens from frost.

Because dew point does not change with air temperature, it is a better indicator of the type of air mass that is situated over the state. In general, there is a very simple way to remember how the dew point will make the air temperature feel. Basically, your discomfort level in the summer depends on the dew point relative to 60°F. When dew points are above that temperature, you notice the humidity and the stickiness. In fact, dew points in the upper 60s, and particularly the low 70s, can make temperatures not normally considered problematic (around 85°F, as an example), to feel quite oppressive. Dew points below 60°F usually mean comfortable conditions.

Although dew point will not vary by a great deal throughout the day, there are large differences in average dew point throughout the year. This difference is a function of the ability of the air to hold water vapor as a function of temperature. Cold air cannot hold as much water vapor so it is generally drier. That is the reason for the abundance of static electricity during the winter. Warmer air can hold more water vapor, so dew points are higher in the summer. Average daily dew points for the state are shown in Figure 8.1. In addition to seasonal changes in dew point, average daily dew point varies across the state. As you might expect, dew points trend higher closer to the coast. In fact, the average winter dew points in the far north range from 5° to 10°F while those along the coast average 15°F. Average summer dew point differences are similar, ranging from the low 50°sF in the north to the mid- to high 50°sF in the south and along coastal areas. There are rare occasions when dew points can top the 70°F mark during the summer, driving even the hardiest Mainers into an air-conditioned building or room. But for the most part, air conditioners are not really that necessary in Maine.

9

SKY CONDITIONS AND FOG

Many times during the year you'll hear Mainers complain about the lack of sun. There are often stretches of 4 to 5 days when cloudy skies dominate the weather. You can get pretty "down in the dumps" during those long periods when the sun fails to make an appearance. Unfortunately, during an average year, Portland receives only 57% of the available sunshine (Table 9.1). The frequency of sunshine is even less farther inland and especially farther north. For instance, Caribou averages 3 to 4 clear days fewer per month than Portland. When it comes to sunshine, Maine is no southwestern state, like Arizona, but its weather is certainly more exciting and the many different cloud formations enhance the lighting and views in the mountains and along the coast. Think about those days when you can see the sun's rays shining through holes in the cloud cover or when the undersides of clouds are picking up the reflected sunlight and producing bright pink and orange tints. Clouds may not be your favorite summertime phenomenon, especially if you're working on a tan, but their presence highlights Maine's scenery. All you have to do is ask a professional photographer.

The cause for the high number of cloudy or at least partly cloudy days is a function of several factors. Most of all, Maine's location relative to circulation patterns in the Northern Hemisphere results in a high number of weather systems moving through or close enough to the state that they influence sky conditions. Almost every storm track across the U. S. converges on Maine. The rising air associated with low-pressure systems as well as the contrast in air masses associated with fronts are both responsible for abundant cloud formation and a high number of cloudy or partly cloudy days.

The northern half of the state and the mountains may see periods of more extensive cloudiness than southern parts because some low-pressure systems may move northward out of the state at very slow speeds. At times, these low-pressure systems seem to "park"

Figure 9.1 Photograph of sea smoke off the coast of Maine. Photo courtesy of John Jensenius, Gray NWS.

themselves for several days, particularly when upper-air patterns (that is the steering currents) are set up in such a way that weather systems are not moving across the country very rapidly. As air moves around these low-pressure systems located north or northeast of the state, it has a tendency to become very unstable, so frequent cloud formation, sometimes with precipitation, will occur across the mountains and the northern part of the state. The mountains enhance the instability as air is forced to move up and over the hills, cooling and forming condensation as it rises.

■ THE SEASONS

Overall, there are more cloudy days throughout the state over the course of the year than either partly cloudy or clear days (Table 9.1). The National Weather Service uses several criteria to quantify these terms: a cloudy day means at least more than 87% of the sky is covered by clouds, a partly cloudy day means 25%–50% of the sky is covered by clouds, and a clear day means either no clouds are observed or 5% or less of the sky is covered by clouds. Between these three commonly used terms are the terms mostly clear, (5%–25% of the sky is covered by clouds), mostly cloudy (50%–69% of the sky is cloud

Table 9.1. Average Number of Cloudy versus Clear Days During the Year for Caribou and Portland

	CARIBOU			PORTLAND			
Month	Cloudy	Partly Cloudy	Clear	Cloudy	Partly Cloudy	Clear	% of Available Sunshine
January	17 (55%)	7 (23%)	7 (23%)	14 (45%)	7 (23%)	10 (32%)	56
February	16 (57%)	6 (21%)	6 (21%)	12 (43%)	7 (25%)	9 (32%)	59
March	17 (55%)	7 (23%)	7 (23%)	15 (48%)	7 (23%)	9 (29%)	56
April	18 (60%)	7 (23%)	5 (17%)	16 (53%)	7 (23%)	7 (23%)	54
May	18 (58%)	9 (29%)	4 (13%)	15 (48%)	10 (32%)	6 (19%)	54
June	17 (57%)	10 (33%)	3 (10%)	13 (43%)	10 (33%)	7 (23%)	59
July	15 (48%)	13 (42%)	3 (10%)	13 (42%)	11 (35%)	7 (23%)	63
August	15 (48%)	11 (35%)	5 (16%)	11 (35%)	11 (35%)	9 (29%)	63
September	15 (50%)	9 (30%)	6 (20%)	12 (40%)	8 (27%)	10 (33%)	62
October	18 (58%)	8 (26%)	5 (16%)	13 (42%)	8 (26%)	10 (32%)	58
November	21 (70%)	6 (20%)	3 (10%)	15 (50%)	7 (23%)	8 (27%)	48
December	19 (61%)	6 (19%)	6 (19%)	15 (48%)	7 (23%)	9 (29%)	53
SEASONAL TOTALS							
Winter	52 (58%)	19 (21%)	19 (21%)	41 (46%)	21 (23%)	28 (31%)	56
Spring	53 (58%)	23 (25%)	16 (17%)	46 (50%)	24 (26%)	22 (24%)	55
Summer	47 (51%)	34 (37%)	11 (12%)	37 (40%)	32 (35%)	23 (25%)	62
Fall	54 (59%)	23 (25%)	14 (15%)	30 (33%)	23 (25%)	28 (31%)	56
Annual	206 (56%)	100 (27%)	59 (16%)	165 (45%)	99 (27%)	101 (28%)	57

Note: Number of days per month with cloudy, partly cloudy, and clear days based on 54 years of record. Cloudy is defined as having >70% cloud cover, partly cloudy (30%-70%), and clear (<30%). Percentage of available sunshine for Portland based on records through 1995. Monthly percentages may not equal 100% because of rounding. Data from www.srh.noaa.gov/tsa/climate/cloud.html.

covered) and considerable cloudiness (70%–87% cloud cover). The annual average varies, however, as northern areas are generally more cloudy than southern coastal parts of the state. Portland, for example, experiences about 100 days (28% of the year) a year with clear skies, yet Caribou averages only 59 days (16% of the year) with clear skies. Both experience the same number of partly cloudy days (about 100, or 28% of the year), but Caribou will have just over 200 cloudy days (56% of the year) compared to the 165 cloudy days (45% of the year) in Portland. So Portland receives about 57% of the available sunshine for the year on average. Caribou would receive less, but that number has not been calculated for Caribou.

Figure 9.2. Photograph of evaporation fog over the Stillwater River, Orono, caused by cold winter air over the warmer river water. Photo by Greg Zielinski.

Winter: While many people may think of dreary winter days with no leaves on the trees and thick clouds in the sky, it is not necessarily the cloudiest season. December is often one of the cloudiest months both inland and along the coast. January has a tendency to be only slightly cloudier than average. However, February, which is the driest month statewide, usually has more clear days and a higher percent of available sunshine than average.

Spring: Overall, spring is the cloudiest season in the state. While it has many cloudy days in The County, based on the records from Caribou, March also has the most clear days of any month. Portland, on the other hand, not only has the most cloudy days in spring, but also has the least number of clear days, with May having the least number of clear days of any month in Portland. Those April clouds and showers are probably a function of the polar front moving northward during the spring.

Summer: Summer sunshine certainly draws tourists into the state. For Caribou the lowest number of cloudy days is recorded in summer, yet summer also has the least number of clear days. This is easily explained as summer heating produces the rising air that leads to afternoon showers and thunderstorms. As so often stated by forecasters during the summer: "there may be pop-up afternoon showers around, but the day will not be a complete washout." In Portland, the most available sunshine is received in summer, especially in July and August. Much like Caribou, the greatest number of partly cloudy days occurs in the summer, as afternoon cloud build-up also is prevalent in the Portland area.

Fall: There is quite a contrast between sky conditions in the north versus the southern coast in the fall. Fall is the cloudiest of the seasons in Caribou and the least cloudy in Portland. Like the spring, part of this may be explained by greater storm activity in the northern part of the state as the polar front begins to move southward. September is the clearest month in Portland, with October close behind. In both Caribou and Portland, November is quite dreary; statewide, it is the wettest month.

■ FOG

Fog is essentially a cloud that forms at ground level, reducing visibility to 0.62 miles (1 km) or less. Fog formation is very common in Maine. Two essential factors lead to fog formation and both of these are common in the region. One is a contrast in temperature between the air and the surface beneath it, which leads to a cooling of the air to the point where condensation occurs immediately above the surface. When enough condensation takes place, the air becomes saturated and a cloud forms at the surface. The second requirement is moist air, and there is no shortage of humidity in Maine, even during the winter.

One of the more common types of fog found across Maine is radiation fog. This forms on clear nights as heat loss (radiational cooling) cools the ground and the air just above the ground. The lowering temperature increases the relative humidity of the air until saturation

Figure 9.3. Fog and cloud cover primarily located over Frenchman Bay as seen from the top of Cadillac Mountain, Acadia National Park. Photo by Chris Zielinski.

is reached and fog begins to form. Gentle winds will help increase the likelihood of fog forming as the process helps mix the moist air near the ground up into the air. Strong winds will mix the air too much and drier air from higher levels will prevent saturation from occurring. The most common type of radiation fog is valley fog. This is the fog that forms in river valleys or valleys with wetlands in their bottoms, a common occurrence in Maine. Cool air sinks into the valley bottom and the moisture is provided by the stream or swampy area.

Interested in predicting whether or not this type of fog will form in the morning? You can get a good idea by knowing the temperature at sunset, the dew

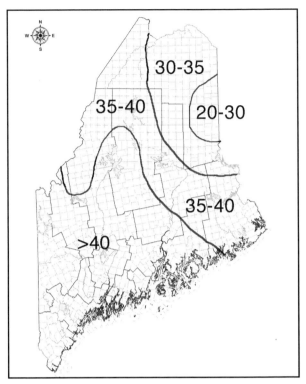

Figure 9.4. Average number of days per year when heavy fog (visibility is <1/4 mile) occurs in Maine.

point, and the wind speed. Most forecasters give this information, as does the Weather Channel and many online sites. There is a good chance radiation fog will occur when the dew point is 9°F below the air temperature and winds are expected to be lower than 5 knots (5.75 mph) (Ackerman and Knox, 2007). Try it and see if you are able to predict the occurrence of fog.

A second type of fog is advection fog. Advection refers to the horizontal movement of air, whereas convection refers to the vertical movement of air. When warm air moves over a cold surface, the air is cooled and the relative humidity of the air increases. This type of fog formation is especially prevalent off the coast when air over warmer water, like the Gulf Stream, moves over the colder water of the Gulf of Maine. This process is responsible for fog over the open waters of the Gulf of Maine. This process is also responsible for fog along the coastline, particularly during fall and spring and sometimes during the winter when the land is colder than the ocean water. Airflow will bring the warmer air from the ocean over the colder land surface, producing advection fog. A similar type of advection fog is prevalent during the summers along the Maine coast. In this scenario, the moist air above the cool ocean moves in over the warmer land surface, increasing the humidity of the air over coastal regions. The result is summer-time fog along the coast.

One frequent method of producing advection fog seems to occur quite often during early spring when there is still a snow cover, although it also can occur during the winter. The key aspect of the process is the movement of warm air over the cold snow pack. The warm air is cooled by the snow pack, becoming saturated and leading to the formation of fog.

The third type of fog present in Maine is primarily a winter phenomenon, especially in coastal bays and harbors. This is evaporation fog, which occurs when warm water evaporates into cold air, saturating the air and forming fog. The most common scenario for this type of fog occurs when very frigid air moves over unfrozen water, particularly along the coastline. The result is the formation of sea smoke, a type of evaporation fog (Fig. 9.1). This type of fog can also show up quite dramatically on satellite images of the open ocean. At times during the winter, a very strong cold front moves through Maine bringing very frigid air with it on strong northwesterly winds. As the cold air moves over the warmer air of the open ocean, dense fog forms. On satellite images, the edge of the fog bank mimics the shape of the shoreline. Evaporation fog may also form over areas of open water on Maine's rivers during the winter (Fig. 9.2).

A final type of fog occurs in the mountains of western Maine. When moist air is forced to move up the slope of a mountain, it will cool and fog may form if it cools to the point of condensation or to the dew point. This is referred to an upslope fog and the process is also responsible for the clouds that may hover around the top of peaks, as often occurs on Mt. Katahdin, keeping the summit shrouded in fog. This process can even occur on smaller mountains, such as Cadillac Mountain. Warm moist air over Frenchman Bay will move up the slopes of Cadillac and keep the summit cloudy and cool compared to conditions in Bar Harbor just below (Fig. 9.3).

The amount of fog recorded annually across the state varies depending on how heavy the fog is and on the resulting visibility. There is no standard scale to measure the type of fog, but if visibility is reduced to 0.25 mile or less, then weather reporters will often call it a heavy or dense fog. Heavy fog is observed in most parts of Maine 30–40 days per year, with the most frequent occurrences along the southern and midcoast regions and into the western mountains (Fig. 9.4). A small section in the eastern part of The County has only 20–30 days of heavy fog.

10

WIND

Sailing, flying kites, and generating electricity are all uses for the wind. Wind can also be very destructive, damaging homes, toppling trees and power lines, and stirring up dangerously high waves. It also can be quite annoying fighting strong crosswinds as you drive down Interstate 95 or paddle your kayak in the Gulf of Maine as the wind drives you away from your destination. You may also curse the wind when an Arctic front drives winter wind chills to sub-zero levels. Walking into the wind at those times may be hazardous due to the risk of frost nip or, in severe cases, frostbite. Wind plays a big part in our day-to-day weather.

Wind is caused by the difference in pressure between air masses—the majority of the wind that we feel is a function of the relationship between high and low-pressure systems at the earth's surface. Much like water, air moves from areas of high-pressure toward areas of low-pressure. However, there is a difference in the nature of this movement. Water under high-pressure will move perpendicular to the lines of equal pressure (called isobars) toward the center of low-pressure. Air movement at the earth's surface is impacted by the Coriolis effect and by friction from the earth's surface. These factors produce airflow that is at an angle to the lines of equal pressure, or isobars, between the high- and low-pressure centers. In general, the combination of all of these features, clockwise airflow around a high-pressure center, counter-clockwise airflow around a low-pressure center, and the angular flow between them essentially produce the regional wind that affects Maine.

In addition to the effect on wind direction by the location of the high- and low-pressure systems, the difference in pressure between the systems (referred to as the pressure gradient) determines wind speed. The greater the difference in pressure, the closer together the isobars on a weather map will be and the greater the wind speeds will be. For example, a very low-pressure nor'easter to the east of Maine combined with very strong high-pressure to the west of the state will generate very strong winds. Sometimes winds under this scenario will require the posting of a high wind advisory by the National Weather Service. The opposite effect is produced when a high-pressure system is located directly over the state. In this case, there is essentially no pressure gradient and winds are calm. This is why the coldest nights during the winter occur a day or two after a storm and the passage of its associated cold front. Wind chills may be greater immediately following the passage of the front because of the strong winds, but actual air temperature will hit rock bottom when the high-pressure system moves directly over the state. The lack of air movement under calm conditions helps produce colder nighttime temperatures because the coldest air at the surface is not able to mix with warmer air just above the surface.

Although circulation patterns determine regional wind direction and speed, wind conditions may not be the same at a given location in the state because the topography of the area also affects the wind. Hills and mountains may block the wind or turn it in a direction that differs from the overall flow across the state. Similarly, the funneling of wind down a valley may increase the average wind speed compared to the overall wind speeds across the state. Wind speeds are also affected by natural wind blocks, such as stands of trees, or by man-made wind blocks, such as buildings and fences. All of these factors can influence how the wind is felt at a single site.

■ SEASONAL WINDS

Probably the type of wind most often talked about by Mainers, and especially by tourists, is the sea breeze. The sea breeze is generated along the coast because the land heats up much quicker than the water. As you might expect, this is most prevalent during the warmer part of the year—late spring through early fall. The sun is at its highest point in the sky at that time so the sunlight reaching the surface is much more effective in heating up the land. Since the water does not heat as quickly, less rising air is generated over water. The rising air over the land creates an area of lower pressure than that over the ocean. Air then moves in off of the ocean to replace the rising air over the land. This flow off the ocean is the sea breeze. To complete the cycle of air movement, the air that rises over the land will move laterally at higher altitudes, cool, and then sink again over the ocean. This creates an area of higher pressure over the ocean, which helps generate more airflow onto the land. This continues until the evening, when the land begins to cool more quickly than the water does, and the flow reverses. So the pattern is a land breeze at night and sea breeze during the day.

The formation of a sea breeze is quite common during the summer, but it's not generated every day. On very cloudy days, the differential heating of the land versus the water is not very great. Consequently, a sea breeze is less likely to form on these days. A very strong regional airflow from the north to northwest to west would also inhibit sea breeze formation. In that case, the flow off of the land is so strong that the pressure difference generated by any differential heating of the land becomes squelched. This was the reason temperatures in coastal areas exceeded 100°F on "Hot Saturday," August 2, 1975 (see

Table 10.1. Average Daily and Average Daily Maximum Wind Speed (mph) for Maine

	Jan	Feb	Mar	Apr	May	Jun	Jul	Aug	Sep	Oct	Nov	Dec	Annual
STATE MONTHLY AVERAGE													
Daily	7.0	7.5	7.9	7.7	6.8	6.1	5.7	5.3	5.8	6.9	7.3	7.2	6.8
Daily Maximum	19.6	21.2	21.5	21.6	19.3	17.7	17.0	15.6	16.2	19.9	20.1	20.8	19.2

STATE SEASONAL AVERAGE			
Winter Daily	7.3	Winter Daily Maximum	20.5
Spring Daily	7.4	Spring Daily Maximum	20.8
Summer Daily	5.7	Summer Daily Maximum	16.9
Fall Daily	6.6	Fall Daily Maximum	18.7

SELECTED INDIVIDUAL MONTHLY AVERAGES													
Caribou	7.5	8.1	8.1	8.5	7.0	6.3	5.8	5.5	6.2	7.5	7.7	8.0	7.2
Frenchville	10.0	10.2	10.3	10.3	8.9	8.3	7.6	7.4	8.4	9.6	9.9	10.0	9.2
Fryeburg	3.9	4.2	4.7	4.9	4.5	4.0	3.6	3.1	3.2	3.9	4.0	3.9	4.0
Bangor	7.7	8.4	9.0	9.0	7.8	7.4	7.0	6.6	6.9	7.7	8.0	7.8	7.8
Augusta	8.3	8.3	9.0	8.8	7.8	7.7	7.4	7.1	7.5	8.5	9.0	8.6	8.2
Bar Harbor	6.7	7.9	8.4	7.8	9.0	6.4	6.0	5.8	6.1	7.3	7.4	7.0	7.2
Wiscasset	4.2	4.8	5.3	5.1	4.5	4.2	3.8	3.5	3.7	4.3	4.6	4.2	4.4
Portland	7.9	8.2	9.2	8.7	7.5	6.9	6.6	6.3	6.5	7.5	7.7	7.8	7.6

Note: Averages in mph determined from automatic weather station (ASOS) data acquired at the airports for various towns around the state listed below for the 7-year period of May 1997–May 2004. Data are unofficial. ASOS data used to determine statewide averages from Augusta, Bangor, Bar Harbor, Brunswick, Caribou, Clayton Lake, Frenchville, Fryeburg, Greenville, Houlton, Lewiston, Millinocket, Portland, Presque Isle, Rockland, Sanford, Waterville, and Wiscasset. Local conditions may play a major role in determining average wind speeds and directions for individual stations.

Chapter 13). It must have been so disappointing to head to the beach on that day and feel no relief from the heat. By contrast, you should remember that the orientation of the coastline of Maine will quite easily allow for the generation of a sea breeze when there is a strong regional flow off the ocean from the south to southwest.

The variety in the weather conditions across the state can also be seen in the prevalent wind conditions. In addition to the variability caused by the ocean's influence, there is a distinct seasonal difference. Wind speeds as a whole are a function of the number of times storms pass close to or through the state, as they set up the large pressure differentials.

Evidence of this variability comes from the distribution of seasonal wind directions for an inland site (Caribou), a more centrally located cite (Bangor), and two sites with a large maritime influence (Portland and Bar Harbor). Average monthly wind speeds from these same stations and several others also highlight the variability throughout the year (Table 10.1).

At the same time, it is worth emphasizing again that wind direction and speed are very much affected by local conditions. Examples highlighting this are the lower wind speeds recorded at Fryeburg and Wiscasset and the higher wind speeds at Frenchville compared to the statewide average (Table 10.1). Several stations, such as Frenchville and Clayton Lake, also show much less seasonal variability in wind direction compared to other locations.

■ WINTER WINDS

The cold conditions of winter are a direct result of the prevalence of northerly winds ranging from the northwest to northeast depending on where you are in the state. The high frequency of northerly winds is a direct function of the number of high-pressure systems that move into the United States from Canada. The actual position and track of the highs determine whether or not the dominant wind direction is more northerly versus northwesterly as do local controls that may exert an influence. Another cause for the prevalence of northeasterly, winds is the frequency of nor'easters during the cold season. The proximity of sites such as Bar Harbor and Portland to these coastal storms probably helps generate the higher frequency of northeasterly winds along the coast compared to more interior and northerly sites.

The impact that coastal storms have on wind direction around the state during the winter also helps explain why average and maximum wind speeds are among the highest of the year. Most sites average a little over 7 mph for daily wind speeds during the winter, with maximum winds averaging more than 20 mph (Table 10.1). More storms are generated during the winter and the greater pressure differences between the storms and adjacent high-pressure systems account for the higher average wind speeds. High-pressure systems are much colder in the winter, which, because very cold air is denser than warm air, also helps produce much stronger highs. The combination of strong highs and strong lows produces the greatest pressure differential and resulting very high-pressure gradient responsible for stronger winds this time of year.

■ SPRING WINDS

Average wind directions and speeds during the spring are similar to those of winter. This is not completely unexpected given that the controls on Maine's spring weather are so similar to the factors that influence winter weather. Most of the state still has a strong northerly wind, or at least the presence of a northerly flow. However, the transition to summer is beginning and that is evident in the additional occurrence of a southerly to southeasterly wind flow.

Figure 10.1. Damage caused by a major wind storm in Maine. Photo courtesy of John Jensenius.

Sites around the state display a very bimodal distribution of wind direction, for example, Bangor shows a dominant wind that varies between almost due north wind and due south. Coastal sites, like Portland, show a great deal of variability, but the most prevalent wind directions likewise are also generally northerly and southerly. Bar Harbor, on the other hand, shows a very strong southwesterly flow, indicating the kind of winds to be expected along the mid- to Down East coasts during the upcoming summer season.

The cause of the bimodal distribution of wind around the state can be explained by the dominant weather controls of the spring months. The presence of a northerly flow reflects the end of the strong Canadian highs moving into the United States and New England. March can be very cold as would occur with these big systems, thus a strong prevalence of northerly winds remains. Later in the spring, the number of Canadian highs lessens and a greater number of highs begin moving across southern parts of the country as the jet stream migrates farther north. High-pressure systems in the south will produce southerly winds in Maine. These more southerly high-pressure systems are a direct function of the increasing strength of the Bermuda High. The sea breeze also begins to show up in late spring, on some very warm days.

Spring wind speeds very much reflect the lingering winter weather patterns (Table

10.1). March is a month that can experience some large nor'easters, some of which are very energized by the pressure gradient set up by powerful Canadian high-pressure systems that follow the storm into New England. In fact, March is the windiest month, on average, for the entire state and April is the second windiest month (Table 10.1). The frequency of large nor'easters is a major factor for spring's windiness, but it is not the only factor. Transition seasons are characterized by a wide variety of circulation patterns that produce pressure gradients capable of generating significant wind speeds. This is the time of year when the position of the jet stream is beginning to migrate northward, enhancing the contrast between circulation systems over the region. More northerly systems, particularly high-pressure systems, will, on average, be stronger than those from the south. The prevalence of significantly contrasting circulation systems helps produce the overall windy conditions of spring.

■ SUMMER WINDS

Summer weather patterns are characterized by much less contrast between circulation systems across the region, which translates into a greater variability in wind patterns except for areas along the coast. Local winds such as the sea breeze and the funneling of winds through river valleys is more likely to be a factor around the state. Generally, however, all areas experience a dominant southerly wind in the summer.

Just as the lack of strong circulation patterns during the summer allows for less dominant wind directions and greater local influence, average wind speeds are also lower during the summer. July and August are the two calmest months of the year, when the average position of the jet stream is north of the state. Overall weaker highs and lows mean less pressure contrast. Thunderstorms can generate high winds, but they are sporadic during the summer, with only a small number of severe thunderstorms in Maine (Chapter 11).

■ FALL WINDS

As you might expect, the wind patterns of fall are similar to those of spring. At the start of fall, the state initially sees patterns that are more similar to those of summer; the winter pattern becomes more evident toward the end of fall. Regardless of the sequence, fall wind patterns, much like spring, are generally characterized by the presence of two predominant wind directions: southerly winds characteristic of the summer pattern, and northerly winds, which are dominant in the winter. Some areas, such as Portland, still experience a high amount of variability in fall winds.

Fall wind patterns reflect the transition of the seasons within the annual cycle. During early fall, specifically during September, overall circulation patterns remain poorly developed, meaning that local winds may have a tendency to be more prevalent than winds generated by well-developed regional patterns. However, as Maine begins to move more and more into the winter pattern, stronger storms and high-pressure systems begin to form. These well-developed circulation patterns lead to more consistent wind patterns and more northerly winds associated with the greater occurrence of Canadian high-pressure systems dropping down into the United States. When these centers are located west and north of the state, Maine is frequently under the influence of northwest winds produced on the east side of the high. Furthermore, the jet stream traverses the state during the fall, bringing a greater frequency of storms across the region. More developed storm systems lead to a greater frequency of specific wind patterns set up by the contrast between high- and low-pressure systems. In addition, nor'easters are again becoming a major part of Maine's weather, particularly as the state progresses into late fall

Average wind speeds especially show the transition from summer to winter and the increasing frequency of well-developed circulation systems (Table 10.1). September is generally a fairly tranquil month, with wind speeds very similar to those of July. By the time fall reaches its peak, wind speeds become more in line with winter and spring. Interestingly, the tropical storm season begins in late August and extends through September, yet these two months have the lowest and third-lowest average wind speeds during the year. Tropical systems do not have a very significant impact on the nature of wind patterns across the state, probably because they are not a very frequent contributor to Maine's weather; and, by the time they do reach Maine, their winds are usually very much diminished. Nor'easters that develop in late October and November can frequently be stronger than tropical systems that reach the area. Furthermore, extra-tropical coastal storms are a much more frequent visitor to the state than tropical systems. Thus, nor'easters have a greater influence on average wind speeds than hurricanes and other tropical systems.

It is important to note that the time period used to determine the average wind conditions discussed in this book is only eight years, compared to the 30-year time frame used to define normal conditions. Unfortunately, widespread wind measurements are not a standard parameter measured under the NWS volunteer program. As a result, wind measurements are not taken across large parts of the state.

11

STORMS

Another of the intriguing aspects of Maine's weather is the variety of storms that can "hit" the state. If you pick a particular type of storm, Maine has probably had one sometime in the recent past. These include thunderstorms, tornadoes, nor'easters, and tropical systems, including both tropical storms and hurricanes. The frequency and magnitude of these storms also vary, with some occurring more often than others, and some of them becoming quite powerful while others gain very little strength. As you read through the information below, you'll note that there is a discussion about an unusual weather phenomenon that is not a storm, but looks a lot like one, and most people would not even associate this type of event with Maine. Intrigued? See the discussion below to find out more.

■ THUNDERSTORMS AND TORNADOES

Thunderstorms form when hot, humid air rises very quickly and with great intensity. There are several processes that initiate rising air. One is simply the continued heating of the land during the day. The process begins with the formation of cumulus clouds, the fluffy white clouds seen on summer days. However, if the air is rising too rapidly, cloud formation continues and these cumulus clouds grow vertically. If conditions allow, the rising air will continue to produce vertical growth of the clouds to the point where a thunderhead or cumulonimbus cloud forms (Fig. 11.1). Because hot, unstable air is the most common air mass for thunderstorm development, these storms occur most frequently on summer afternoons as the heat has built up over the course of the day. Another process that produces thunderstorms is the lifting of air caused by an approaching frontal system, especially when a cold front moves into a very hot and humid air mass

Figure 11.1. Photograph of the vertical development of two thunderstorms or cumulonimbus clouds east of Bangor. Time between the two photos is roughly 15 minutes. The white line gives a perspective on the amount of vertical growth that occurred for the two developing thunderheads. Photo by Greg Zielinski.

over the state. Both of these processes may force hot, humid air up the slopes of the hills and mountains of western Maine, enhancing the cooling of the air, cloud formation, and possible thundershower formation. This is one reason why there are often showers in the mountainous areas of the state, but not elsewhere. The lightning associated with afternoon thunderstorms in the mountains can be very dangerous to hikers and backpackers if they do not take precautions to reduce the likelihood of being hit by lightning.

When it comes to these storms, Maine holds an interesting position in the United States. On average, Maine has the fewest days with thunderstorms during the year than any other state east of the Rocky Mountains. Most of the state only has about 20 days per year when a thunderstorm occurs, although there may be more than one thunderstorm on those days. The 20-per-year line basically cuts the state in half, with northern and eastern parts, particularly Down East and coastal areas, having fewer than 20 days per year, and western and southern parts of the state away from the coast having more than 20 days per year with a thunderstorm.

The reason Maine has so few thunderstorms compared to the rest of the eastern two-thirds of the country is two-fold. One reason is the northerly location of the state. Moist, hot air is one ingredient that leads to thunderstorm formation and an air mass of that type does not make it into Maine that often. It is true that Maine gets an influx of hot, humid air during the summer, but it does not occur with the same frequency as in other parts of the eastern United States. In addition, it takes a while for this type of air to make its way into Maine with enough regularity for thunderstorm formation to become a common occurrence. In fact, it is not until mid- to late summer when this occurs. Consequently, most thunderstorms occur in Maine during late July and August. The second explanation for limited thunderstorm formation is also the primary reason for the low numbers of these storms in coastal areas. The development of the sea breeze brings cool, stable air into near-shore areas, replacing the hot, humid unstable air that provides the fuel for thunderstorm growth. This is also why severe thunderstorms rarely occur in coastal regions. The cooler, more stable air along the coast will not rise with the great intensity needed to form severe thunderstorms.

Although severe thunderstorms are rare across the state, they do occasionally occur. A severe thunderstorm, as defined by the National Weather Service, is characterized by winds at least 58 mph (50 knot) with the possibility of at least 3/4-inch hail. The most likely cause of a severe thunderstorm in Maine is a strong cold front that moves into very unstable (hot and humid) air over the state. This scenario may occur when Maine has been under the influence of a strong southwesterly airflow around a stationary high-pressure system located south of the state. One feature of a severe or very strong thunderstorm may be hail. Hail is made up of concentric layers of ice that form in the great updrafts and downdrafts within a strong to severe thunderstorm. Water droplets are pushed upward on strong updrafts and freeze as they reach higher, colder air. They may then fall in a downdraft, partially melting and accumulating more water around the drop. As they encounter an adjacent updraft, they may once again be pushed upward, refreezing. The whole process continually adds ice to the exterior of the hailstone until it is too heavy to be carried upward and falls out of the cloud. Because severe thunderstorms are not common in Maine, hail is also not a common occurrence. For instance, hail that reaches 1/4-inch in diameter occurs less than once per year across most of Maine (Fig. 11.2). Southwestern parts of the state may receive hail of this size, on average, once per year.

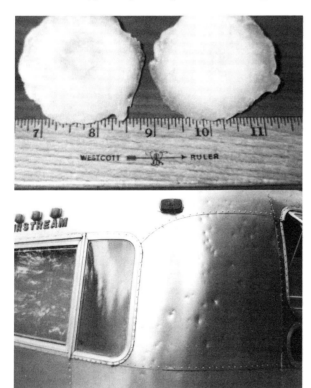

Figure 11.2. Photograph of large hailstones (top) from a thunderstorm near Springfield, Maine on Juy 19, 1995. Hail rarely gets this large in the state. Bottom photo shows the resulting damage to a trailer from the storm. Photos courtesy of John Jensenius, Gray NWS.

Given that severe thunderstorms are rare, it is natural that tornadoes also occur rarely in the state. Tornadoes are associated with severe thunderstorms as the vertical up and down air movement can be vigorous enough that a tornado

Figure 11.3. Tree damage associated with the F-2 tornado that touched down near the west shore of Cobbosseecontee Lake on July 8, 1996. Winds were estimated to be about 130 mph. Photos courtesy of John Jensenius, Gray NWS.

will form. On average, Maine has about two reported tornadoes per year. The intensities of these are usually very low; they will rarely be above an F0 (40–73 mph) or F1 (74–112 mph) on the Fujita Tornado Intensity Scale, the scale used to classify tornadoes. Although tornadoes are more likely to occur in interior southwestern Maine, they can occur almost anywhere (Fig. 11.3). They are most rare along the coast, especially Down East.

On the other hand, severe to almost severe thunderstorms can cause damage from straight-line winds, and in reality, most wind damage from thunderstorms in Maine is probably due to straight-line winds. These are very fast moving downdrafts—cold air parcels that leave the storm and spread out as they hit the ground. Another name for these straight-line winds is microburst, and, if moving fast enough, they can produce high wind speeds. Microbursts can easily reach speeds above 100 mph, so they can generate significant amounts of damage; they just lack the rotation of a tornado. In fact, these downdrafts can often be felt before a line of severe thunderstorms reaches an observer. You may have noticed that as a strong thunderstorm or series of storms approaches, with the very dark gray sky covering the entire horizon, winds will pick up significantly. These are the downdrafts leaving the approaching thunderstorm and they are referred to as a gust front.

■ DUST DEVILS

Perhaps the first thing you think of when you hear the term dust devil is the desert, as in southern Arizona. Well, dust devils can and do occur in Maine. Unfortunately, one that occurred on May 19, 2003 was large enough that it caused some damage and a fatality. Although a dust devil is not a storm, its appearance conjures up thoughts of tornadoes—a swirling mass of wind that is visible because of the dust and debris it picks up. So how do dust devils form in Maine?

A dust devil forms when heating of the surface by the sun causes air to rise. The rising column of air then begins to spin by some mechanism such as differing winds aloft or possibly by moving past an obstacle or irregularity on the ground, such as a building or small high spot on the surface. If the heating causes the air to rise faster and faster, the spin may become faster and more intense to the point where it starts to pick up dust. Dust devils are usually only a few feet in diameter and less than 100 feet in height; but they have been known to spread to a width of 300 yards and a height of more than 1,000 feet. Most dust devils last less than 15 minutes, though they have been known to last more than an hour.

The weather on May 19, 2003 was clear and warm, with a high of 81°F in Sanford. Sustained winds were not strong, averaging 3.5 mph in Sanford, but peak gusts up to 17 mph were recorded. A dust devil formed in the town of Lebanon, and at 12:20 in the afternoon it ran into the two-story Vintage Auto Body shop. This particular dust devil was large enough that it apparently lifted the roof off the building, causing it to collapse and kill the owner of the shop. Another individual was able to dive under a car to avoid serious injury. Fatalities caused by dust devils in the United States are extremely rare, but this incident further highlights the great diversity of Maine's weather.

■ NOR'EASTERS

Of the major storms that affect Maine, the type that undoubtedly has the greatest overall impact from year to year is the nor'easter. Nor'easters can occur in almost any month, although they are rare in July and less common in June and August. Nevertheless, the potential for a significant nor'easter hitting Maine or having an indirect impact on the state exists about nine months of the year. Thunderstorms may occur in any month (yes, there can be thunder snowstorms), but thunderstorms are most common from May through September, and severe thunderstorms with associated tornadoes are most likely to happen in July and August. Tropical storms are generally limited to the very end of summer

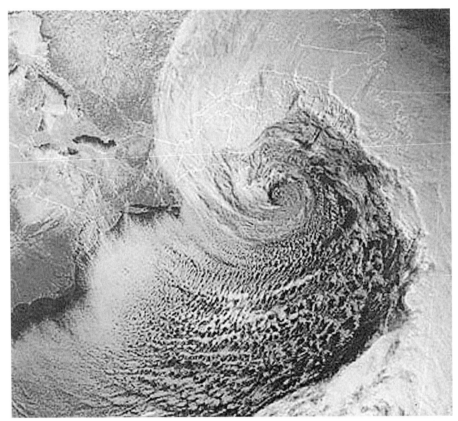

Figure 11.4. Satellite image of a large nor'easter that moved over Maine in January of 2000. The storm was very intense, with a central low-pressure of 948 mb, which produced the eye shown on the image. The cold front is marked by the huge cloud bank southeast of the low. The dry slot is noted by the limited number and extent of clouds moving into the center of the storm. Image provided by Hendricus Lulofs, NWS Caribou.

and earliest fall. So, nor'easters are the "winners" as far as the most common type of major storm to occur in Maine.

Depending on the storm track and time of year, Nor'easters can produce significant amounts of precipitation in the form of snow, sleet, freezing rain, and rain. Some of the more intense storms easily produce heavy precipitation (some very intense nor'easters have been known to produce easily more than 2 inches of snow per hour) and hurricane-force winds that lead to great amounts of drifting and blizzard conditions during the winter, as well as significant coastal erosion from wave action and coastal flooding, particularly during periods of high tide.

Nor'easters are very complex low-pressure systems that form with the interaction of warm, moist air from off the ocean, cold, moist air from the northeast, and dry, cold air coming in from the northwest. They often have a classic comma shape to them when viewed by satellite, the head of the comma representing the clouds around the low-pressure system and the tail of the comma indicating the clouds formed by the cold front that extends from the central low (Fig. 11.4). The tail is highlighted by dry, cloud-free air that gets incorporated into the low, that is, the dry slot.

The number of nor'easters that impact Maine can vary widely from year to year. As many as 20–30 will form each cold season off the east coast of the United States, and, in some years, 10–15 may eventually move far enough up the coast to have a major impact on Maine. They are a prominent player in Maine's weather and climate. In fact, five of Maine's largest weather events of the last 200 years are, in my opinion, nor'easters.

■ TROPICAL SYSTEMS

As late summer approaches, many eyes along the east coast of the United States look toward the tropics. The great impact of tropical storm systems on the entire eastern and southeastern third of the country is indisputable. These are the largest and most powerful storms that exist on earth, so it is no wonder that anyone living on the eastern seaboard pays attention to the forecasts when a hurricane approaches. Although the southeastern U. S. is more susceptible to landfall by a major hurricane, Maine is certainly not immune to the impact from a tropical system.

Tropical systems that affect Maine come under five different categories (Table 11.1). The most obvious is direct landfall by a hurricane. Hurricane status is reached when

Table 11.1. Average Frequency of the Different Types of Tropical-based Storm Systems that Affect Maine and the Gulf of Maine.

Type of System	Average Frequency
All tropical-based systems	1 every 1.5 yrs or 2 every 3 years
Tropical-based systems that cross the state	1 every 3 years
All landfall systems	1 every 8 years
Landfall tropical systems	1 every 12 years
Landfall hurricanes	1 every 33 years

Note: Based on records from 1851 through 2007 as available from National Hurricane Center home page, www.nhc.noaa.gov/. Definitions for various types of systems as follows.

All tropical-based systems: Includes 1) tropical systems (both hurricanes and tropical storms) that make landfall in Maine, 2) tropical systems that make landfall outside of Maine, but then travel up the coast and move through Maine, 3) tropical systems that change to extratropical low-pressure systems (transitional storms) and either make landfall in Maine or elsewhere and travel through the state, and 4) tropical systems and transitional storms that travel through the Gulf of Maine, but do not make landfall in Maine or cross the state.

Tropical-based systems that cross the state: Includes types 1 and 2 from above, plus transitional storms that travel through the state.

All landfall systems: Includes type 1 from above, plus transitional storms that make landfall in Maine.

Landfall tropical systems: Includes type 1 from above.

Landfall hurricanes: Includes only storms that are at hurricane status at the time of landfall.

maximum sustained winds reach 74 mph (64 knots). The second category is direct land-fall of a tropical storm. Tropical storms have maximum sustained winds between 39 and 73 mph (34 and 63 knots). The third category is also probably the most likely to affect Maine. It is the tropical system (hurricane or tropical storm) that makes landfall somewhere else along the east coast or even the coast of the Gulf of Mexico, but which then moves northeastward into Maine as a low-pressure system. Tropical systems can also changes their characteristics to be more of a mid-latitude or extra-tropical storm. The last category is when any of these different types of tropical systems move through the Gulf of Maine, potentially into the Canadian Maritimes, without directly crossing the state. Nevertheless, the storm may be large enough that it still impacts the state, and, of particular importance, it will have a significant impact on coastal areas and on people working on or just enjoying the Gulf of Maine.

Tropical systems develop in warm ocean waters and the storms that eventually reach Maine primarily form in the equatorial Atlantic. The Gulf of Mexico also is a major area of hurricane development in the Atlantic Basin, but those storms move across land before they have any impact on Maine. There are two primary criteria in the development of a tropical system. The first is an ocean temperature of at least 80°F. At this temperature, the warm waters evaporate rapidly and there is an abundance of rising air, or convection. As in all storm formation, the rising air cools, condenses, and forms clouds. As the process continues, the clouds grow vertically, forming clusters of thunderstorms. When ocean temperatures fall below 80°F there is not enough convection to form or maintain these extensive clusters of thunderstorms. Consequently, the warm ocean waters provide the fuel for hurricane growth. The second component is for these thunderstorms to form a circulation pattern, like a low-pressure system. This is where the Coriolis effect comes into play. This is the force generated by the earth's shape and its rotation. The effect causes low-pressure systems in the Northern Hemisphere to have a counter-clockwise motion to them and high-pressure systems to have a clockwise motion to them. The Coriolis effect causes these thunderstorm clusters to begin circulating in a counter-clockwise motion, resulting in a distinct center of circulation. Initially, this process forms a tropical depression with sustained winds of less than 39 mph (34 knots). If environmental conditions are appropriate, continued convection and thunderstorm development around this circulation may eventually lead to a distinct grouping of massive thunderstorms and increased wind speeds at the surface. Once sustained wind speeds reach 39 mph, the depression is given tropical storm status and is named by the National Hurricane Center in Florida. Once a storm reaches this level, it may have a circulation that is developed well enough to form an eye. If conditions remain favorable, the storm will continue to strengthen, eventually reaching hurricane status. The intensity of a hurricane, based on maximum sustained wind speeds and the central pressure, is then classified according to the Saffir-Simpson Hurricane Intensity Scale, with a Category 1 being the weakest hurricane and a Category 5 hurricane being the strongest. Any hurricane of Category 3 or greater is considered a major hurricane.

The tropical storms and hurricanes that are most likely to affect Maine will usually form around the Cape Verde Islands in the eastern Atlantic Ocean off the northwestern coast of Africa. These systems will move westward toward the Americas on the easterly trade winds. As they approach the Caribbean Sea and the Americas they may continue westward toward Central America or begin to curve northwestward into the Gulf of Mexico. Sometimes they migrate up the central part of the Atlantic or move toward the east coast of the United States. This northwestward curve forms as the storm moves around the subtropical Bermuda High. Storms that approach the eastern seaboard of the United States may then move into coastal areas of the southeast or mid-Atlantic states or remain offshore until they reach New England and Maine. The exact track a hurricane takes will be controlled by the strength and position of any weather systems moving across the United States and the strength and position of the subtropical high in the Atlantic. Regardless of the track taken, as the storm moves northward it will begin to weaken because it will move over progressively cooler water. This is why any hurricane that reaches Maine will be, at most, a Category 3 hurricane. Hurricanes are usually Category 2 or less by the time they get this far north. Hurricanes also gain speed as they move north through the mid-latitudes.

The impact from tropical systems is three-fold. Although wind damage is not as much of a concern in Maine as in areas farther south, because most tropical systems have weakened by the time they reach the state, wind damage can still occur, as gusts may easily be above 100 mph, even with a minimum-strength hurricane. The greatest damage from wind is usually the felling of trees and branches onto power lines and the loss of electricity over widespread areas. Winds of even tropical storm strength (39–73 mph) are more likely to uproot trees when the ground is saturated from heavy rains.

The second potential impact from a tropical system as it makes landfall comes from the storm surge, an increase in water levels along the coast. Water levels rise for two reasons. As a storm approaches landfall in an area like Maine, the winds are circulating in a counter-clockwise pattern. These winds will push water ahead along the northeast quadrant of the storm, where the winds are the strongest and the average height of the water along the coast will increase. In addition, the very low-pressure of a tropical system allows water levels to increase in height simply because there is not as much air pressing down on the water. The amount of water-level increase from this process is not great (1 foot of water for every 0.89 inches of mercury or 30 millibar drop in sea-level pressure), but when added to the wind-driven increase in water level, it may be enough to flood certain areas of the coastline not ordinarily prone to flooding. Adding to the flooding potential and erosion along the shore are the high waves on top of the storm surge. Also, a hurricane making landfall at high tide would likely enhance coastal damage. As a result, maximum coastal damage (flooding and wave erosion) will occur along the northeast side of a tropical system that comes onshore at high tide.

Although the impact from the wind and storm surge may be dramatic, the greatest impact felt in Maine by a tropical system will be heavy rain and the flooding that results. Wind speeds and storm surge along with the resulting damage are dramatically lower in Maine than with hurricanes that make landfall in southeastern states, but these tropical systems sill carry copious amounts of moisture with them. For instance, a large number of the greatest rainfall events in New England are associated with tropical systems such as the 25-plus inches received in Westfield, Massachusetts, from Hurricane Diane in August 1955. Rainfall amounts of 3–5 inches are quite common in Maine from tropical systems. It is very hard for streams and rivers to remain within their banks when they must carry all that water landing in their drainage basins over a 12- to 24-hour period, or possibly over even a shorter time period. One particularly heavy rainfall from a tropical system was the 8 inches from Hurricane Edna that fell over a 24-hour period in Brunswick on September 11, 1954.

Tropical systems can have a major impact on Maine, but at times there is just as much of an impact from storms that begin as a hurricane or tropical system, but by the time they reach Maine they have the characteristics of a typical low-pressure system of the mid-latitudes. This transition from tropical to extra-tropical storm is quite an interesting phenomenon and is a fascinating field of study for meteorologists. It is just one way that these two major storm types are associated with each other. Another is the interaction between two separate systems that exist at the same time. In fact, this second situation has probably occurred in two of the top Maine weather events discussed later in Chapter 13.

12

THE MARINE FORECAST

Many people preparing to venture onto the Gulf of Maine eagerly listen to the radio or television for the marine forecast. This holds true not only for lobstermen and fishermen, but also for recreational users as well. In fact, it was noted at the "Lobstah" exhibit at the Penobscot Marine Museum in Searsport, during the summer and fall of 2004, that one local lobsterman turns on the National Oceanic and Atmospheric Administration (NOAA) marine radio forecast first thing in the morning. When your livelihood—and life—is so dependent on weather conditions, checking the forecast becomes one of the most important items in your daily routine. The marine forecast is especially important because weather conditions may be markedly different than those on land, and even quite different than conditions along the immediate coast. Temperature, precipitation, wind and resulting wave conditions (height and period), and visibility are a few weather conditions that play a critical role in the safety of those on the water. Other aspects of the weather may also be quite different on the water, but they may not be as critical a safety issue. Here are some key aspects about what the marine forecast may be telling us.

■ THE INFORMATION

Often one of the problems in determining what the weather is doing at sea is the lack of any type of weather station. Luckily, information can be gotten from a couple of sources. One source is from ships, and for the Gulf of Maine that means from lobstermen. The other source is buoys that collect various atmospheric and oceanic data (Fig. 12.1). In the case of the Gulf of Maine, there are two sets of buoys that can help forecasters and mariners understand existing weather conditions and forecast future conditions. The two groups that have deployed buoys on the Gulf of Maine are NOAA and the Gulf of

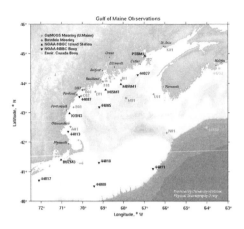

Figure 12.1. Location of buoys (left) in the Gulf of Maine and a close-up photograph (right) of one of those buoys. Map and picture from the GoMoos Web site (www.gomoos.org) and used with permission from Neal Pettigrew (GoMoos chief scientist and professor of oceanography, University of Maine). Photo taken by Neal Pettigrew.

Maine Ocean Observing System (GoMOOS), a federally funded program headquartered in Portland in cooperation with individuals from the School of Marine Sciences at the University of Maine. One of the intriguing aspects of these buoys that is most beneficial to fishermen and recreational boaters is that data are available online in real time. Consequently, you can check existing weather conditions at the locations of any of the buoys from these two networks. Visibility, however, is only available from the GoMOOS buoys. The Web site at the time of this writing for the NOAA buoy system is www.ndbc.noaa. gov, and the GoMoos Web site is www.gomoos.org. The type of data available includes atmospheric conditions such as temperature, wind direction and speed, and water conditions, including water temperature at the surface and at various depths, and wave height and period. Examples of the information available from the Web in near real-time are shown in Figure 12.2.

■ TEMPERATURE

Water has a much greater heat capacity; it does not heat up as quickly as land nor does it cool off as quickly. As a result, the yearly distribution of air temperatures over the Gulf of Maine has a much lower range from summer highs to winter lows than many stations inland. An example of the yearly air temperature distribution comes from the Eastern Maine Shelf buoy. Maximum summer temperature is in the high 50s°F and the lows in January of 2004 dropped into the teens. Temperatures are similar in Casco Bay, where the summer maximum was in the low 60s°F in the summer of 2004 and winter lows were in the high teens. The Gulf of Maine is also dominated by the inflow of water from the Labrador Current (Figs. 12.3 and 3.1). This cold water helps keep water temperatures in the gulf quite low compared to other sites along the east coast. The cool water temperatures mean that the Gulf of Maine is not a significant heat source for the air above it.

■ PRECIPITATION

There are probably two major differences between precipitation characteristics over the Gulf of Maine compared with over interior parts of Maine. One is simply the presence of precipitation on open water versus inland. This may be especially true with storms approaching from mid-Atlantic areas and moving toward the northeast. Sometimes precipitation from these storms may wrap around into the Gulf of Maine, and into Nova Scotia, but not reach Maine. Precipitation from storms that move through the St. Lawrence River Valley may not reach far enough to the south and east to affect the gulf. The major movement of storms from west to east, and particularly from northwest to southeast, as may occur with an approaching cold front, will usually move showers and a major rain

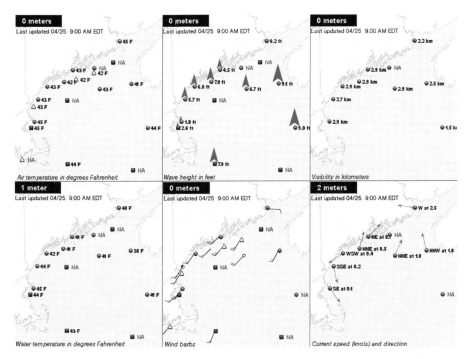

Figure 12.2. Example of near real-time atmospheric and oceanic conditions available from buoys in the Gulf of Maine as obtained at the GoMoos Web site (www.gomoos.org).

shield from off the land and onto the water. The second primary difference may be the intensity of summer showers or thunderstorms. In many cases, because these storms derive much of their energy from the rising air associated with the heating of the land, they may dissipate or weaken as they move over the cool waters of the gulf. Because buoys in the gulf do not collect precipitation amounts regularly, there is not an abundance of data to give specific examples.

■ WIND

It's pretty clear why there are so many sailboats on the Gulf of Maine during the summer; it's the frequency of brisk winds. Wind speeds over the ocean are greater than those on land because there is nothing to disrupt the flow of the wind over the open water. On land, hills and other features on the landscape, as well as buildings and trees, will block the wind or cause enough friction to slow it down. So you'll often hear that wind speeds in a marine forecast are greater than those given for land. The greatest wind speeds will occur with major storms, particularly during the winter or when tropical systems reach the gulf during late summer. In general, wind speeds are lower during the summer, although winds often increase over the course of a summer day as the land heats up and the sea breeze kicks in. Winds on the open water die down during the evening and overnight. Records from the Gulf of Maine indicate that average wind speeds vary from around 5 knots during late summer to around 15 knots or higher during the cold season, as recorded by buoys from Casco Bay and from the Eastern Maine Shelf.

Prevalent wind directions on the Gulf of Maine are similar to those recorded along the immediate coast. Winter months are dominated by more northerly winds, with the classical northeast winds during major storms. During the summer months, southwesterly winds are much more prevalent.

■ VISIBILITY

If you're venturing onto the ocean, one of the most important atmospheric conditions that you'll need to be aware of is visibility. Fog forms easily over open water as warm, humid air moves over the cool ocean. The ocean waters are cool enough to cause the air temperature to drop far enough for condensation of water vapor to occur. The fog formed in this case is referred to as advection fog, and it can occur quite frequently during the summer. A problem, especially for recreational boaters and kayakers in particular, is that this fog can move into shallow waters and onto the immediate coastline quite quickly. What began as a sunny, beautiful day may quickly change to a dangerous situation as visibility is reduced to almost nothing over a very short period of time. Fog in the form of sea smoke can also be quite common during the winter months, particularly in near-shore areas. In this case, cold, Arctic air moves over the warmer ocean waters creating an ideal situation for fog formation. The process occurring under this scenario is the reverse of what happens in summer. It usually only happens on especially frigid

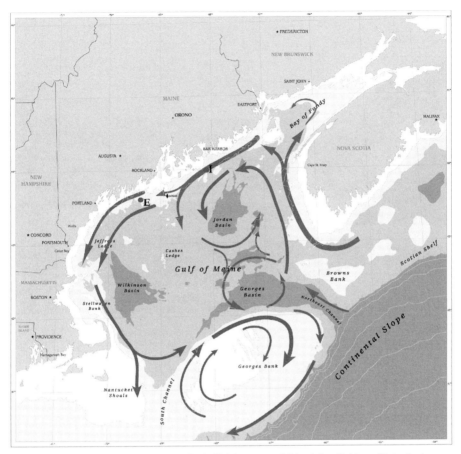

Figure 12.3. Dominant currents in the Gulf of Maine as available at the GoMoos Web site (www. gomoss.org).

mornings, when warmer air just above the water gets cooled by the very cold air flowing off the land. This lowers the temperature of the moisture-laden air to the condensation point, resulting in the formation of fog.

■ WATER CONDITIONS

Conditions on the gulf play an integral part in what is happening or is going to happen to the air above it and ultimately, weather conditions as a whole. On the other hand, existing atmospheric conditions play a huge role in what is happening to the water. The two most obvious water characteristics that reflect what is going on in the atmosphere are temperature and wave conditions. There is a very active and ongoing feedback mecha-

Figure 12.4. Photograph of a large wave breaking ashore on Great Head, Acadia National Park. The abundant large waves along the coast that day were generated by a hurricane well offshore. Photo by Greg Zielinski.

nism between the ocean and the atmosphere, meaning that a change in atmospheric conditions can cause a change in oceanic conditions, which may then alter the original atmospheric conditions. The same would hold true for a change in the initial ocean conditions and their effect on the atmosphere and the eventual response of the ocean to that change in the atmosphere. This relationship between ocean and atmosphere ultimately may play a huge role in weather conditions on land, particularly along the coast. For instance, the warm air over the ocean may move inland during a nor'easter, ultimately changing the snow to sleet, freezing rain, or rain in certain areas, depending on the storm track.

Surface water temperatures, as well as temperatures in the upper levels of the water column, are directly related to air temperature, particularly to depths where sunlight can penetrate. Beyond that depth, atmospheric temperatures have little or no impact on water temperatures. Although the amount of heating from the sun and atmosphere has a direct effect on the resulting surface temperature in the Gulf of Maine, the movement of currents also plays a role. It is, in fact, the interaction of water from the Scotian Shelf, possibly some from the cold Labrador Current, and from the inshore edge of the Gulf Stream, that help dictate the ultimate temperature distribution of the water column. Nevertheless, sea-surface temperatures (SST) in the Gulf of Maine vary from the upper 30s°F in the winter months to the low to mid-60s°F by early September, as observed for 2002 and 2003 in Casco Bay.

Wave conditions, especially wave heights, are a direct function of wind conditions and atmospheric circulation patterns not only over the Gulf of Maine, but also over large parts of the North Atlantic. Large waves or swells frequently move through the Gulf of Maine from storm systems out in the open ocean (Fig. 12.4). These include both extra-tropical storms and quite frequently hurricanes. Very often a hurricane will be as far south as Bermuda, yet can generate large swells that affect the entire eastern seaboard. These large waves also help rip current formation, which leads to warnings and, unfor-tunately, the occasional death of thrill seekers playing in the large waves. Wave heights generally fall into the 2- to 5-foot range, but during large storms they can reach more than 10 ft. Wave heights vary throughout the Gulf of Maine at any given time, so those numbers are average for one particular site. One of the largest waves recorded in the outer reaches of the Gulf of Maine occurred during the Hallows Eve Storm of 1991 (that is, "The Perfect Storm"). One buoy located off Georges Bank recorded a wave height on the order of 39 feet (www.ncdc.noaa.gov).

Changing air circulation patterns in the North Atlantic also influence the direction of wave propagation. Prevalent wind directions on the Gulf of Maine are very much similar to those recorded along the coast, ranging from more variable, with a greater frequency of northern winds, during cool seasons to a strong south to southwesterly flow during the summer months. Wave directions and heights produced by these winds respond accord-ingly. Because of the impact wave heights and direction can have on maritime activities as well as on properties along the immediate coast, wave forecasts are also available from the GoMoos Web site (www.gomoos.org).

13

THE BIG EVENTS

Weather lore probably contributes the most to our continuing fascination with Maine's weather. Much of that lore originates with extreme weather events, those events whose impacts are so great that stories are passed down from generation to generation. Given the tremendous diversity of Maine's weather, there are a several weather events that stand out. These are newsworthy events that dominate the discussion at the local coffee shop or general store for days after. These events also reappear in the media on their 10-, 25-, even 50-year anniversaries. After all, characteristic of Mainers is the ability to talk about a major hardship in an almost nonchalant manner.

But what makes a weather event a newsworthy or extreme event? Big storms are obvious, including hurricanes, tornadoes, and their associated thunderstorms, ice storms, and, of course, nor'easters, including nor'easters that are either major rain or snow events. Other types of events, however, could be newsworthy because they occur over longer periods of time; a classic example is a drought. Heat waves and cold spells also may fit, although a single very hot or cold day can be a significant event for an individual or community. It can be difficult to define or select which events deserve to be labeled as one of Maine's top ten. In reality, the criterion used to judge weather events is a matter of perspective. The two main perspectives most often used are to look at the event from a meteorological perspective or from an impact perspective—that is the overall effect a given event had on the people of Maine.

In the meteorological perspective, you would label an event as being extreme or significant if its magnitude or intensity is truly outstanding compared to most storms or events of similar type. The time factor, however, is very important for considering an event based on its intensity. A storm or event of a particular intensity is more likely to be anomalous when only compared to storms of the past decade or two, rather than looking back over the last century. That same storm may not stand out as significantly when compared to storms over a longer time frame. In some cases, the opposite may be true, when a storm or event seems to have greater impact when compared to the impacts of events over only a short period of time.

There are times when a storm or event would not be considered an extreme weather event based on its magnitude, but it had a significant impact on some aspect of society. Potential reasons for a major impact from a weaker storm may be that the storm was slow moving, so it brought a prolonged period of precipitation; or the core of the storm was centered over a more populated area.

Keeping these ideas in mind, here is a list of Maine's top ten weather events for roughly the last 200 years, with a brief list of several honorable mentions, followed by an overview of each event. Lists like this are quite subjective, but if anything comes from them it may be a lot of discussion and friendly arguments.

1) **Ice Storm of January 1998**

2) **100-Hour Snowstorm, February 1969**

3) **Rains of October 1996**

4) **All Hallow's Eve Storm (aka "The Perfect Storm"), October 1991**

5) **Drought of 2001**

6) **Hot Saturday, August 1975**

7) **Blizzard of December 1962**

8) **Droughts of the late 1940s and mid-1960s (a tie!)**

9) **S.S. *Portland* Gale, November 1898**

10) **Groundhog Day Storm, 1976**

Honorable Mentions: Saxby's Gale, October 1869; winter cold of 1970–1971; floods of 1987; "Year Without a Summer", 1816; and the Maine hurricane of your choice.

EVENT 1 ■ ICE STORM, JANUARY 1998

No matter what criteria are used to determine the top weather event in Maine, the ice storm of January 5–10, 1998 is a truly worthy candidate. The amount of icing associated with this storm may not have been as great as other, more localized ice storms, but the thickness of the ice over such a large part of the state and its subsequent impact make this storm the top Maine weather event of the last 200 years.

The meteorological conditions that led to Ice Storm '98 can be best described as stagnant. As summarized by DeGaetano (2000), surface conditions were characterized by a

Figure 13.1. Photographs of damage associated with the ice storm of 1998. Photographs courtesy of William Sneed.

stationary front that oscillated across the northeastern United States from January 5–10 1998. Cold air remained at the surface north of the front, while warm air was at the surface to the south. Waves of low-pressure moved along the front on the 8th and 9th, causing periods of enhanced precipitation across the region. A key component in the storm was a strong southerly flow at upper levels of the atmosphere that carried warm air and abundant moisture from the Gulf of Mexico. The persistence of warm air at upper levels and cold, sub-freezing air at the surface north of the front provided ideal conditions for frequent periods of freezing rain and significant accumulation of ice. Freezing rain was recorded continuously in Bangor from late January 4 through most of January 6, with long periods of freezing rain again through most of January 7 and 8. Temperatures did not climb above freezing until January 10, when the frontal system finally moved through Maine.

The thickness of ice accumulation across the state was an inch or more, with total precipitation amounts generally between 2 and 3 inches (5.5 to 7.5 cm) That amount of ice is more than enough to topple trees and snap limbs (Fig. 13.1). Evidence of the ice storm could still be seen more than seven years after the storm in bent birch trees. Falling trees, portions of tree trunks, and branches all contributed to downed power lines. The accumulated weight of the ice on power lines also lead directly to their collapse, as well as to the breaking of poles and telephone lines. Although the ice thickness and the overall amount of icing from the '98 storm has been exceeded by other storms over the last few decades, those storms were more localized, so the extent of damage was much less widespread.

The loss of electricity, for as long as a few weeks in some cases, forced many people to resort to other means for heating their homes. The use of woodstoves increased dramatically, which—combined with improperly vented generators—may be the reason for the large number of cases of carbon monoxide poisoning that resulted from the storm. Some feel that this might represent the greatest number of carbon monoxide poisoning cases ever recorded from a single event in the United States (DeGaetano, 2000). After the storm, there was period of time when smoke from woodstoves and fireplaces was recorded as an observable atmospheric condition in Bangor.

Many questions have come up about the potential causes of the ice storm and what they may mean for the future. Foremost is the idea that the exceptionally strong El Niño of that winter was responsible for the formation of the ice storm. After all, it seemed as though every type of weather that winter was blamed on El Niño by the media. In reality, El Niño's role in the '98 ice storm was not a direct but more of a general influence on the event. The influence came from the general global circulation patterns in existence at the time, which were influenced by El Niño. So, while regional or local circulation patterns— those leading to the formation of the ice storm—were influenced by El Niño, the El Niño did not directly cause the event.

Global warming has also been discussed as a potential cause of the ice storm. The idea is that with continued warming, the region will see more of this type of ice storm. But the factors that led to the ice storm could happen anytime; they do not require the slightly warmer temperatures of recent years. In fact, the potential for a significant ice storm occurs with many storms each winter. While the wide extent of the event outside of Maine would not occur with most nor'easters, a major ice storm may develop with certain coastal systems, or when overall circulation patterns do not change very rapidly.

EVENT 2 ■ 100-HOUR STORM, SNOWSTORM OF FEBRUARY 1969

The name of this storm immediately explains why this was such a significant snowstorm in Maine and much of eastern New England. The initial storm formed on February 22 in the Gulf of Mexico and its impact on the United States did not cease for another six days. Snowfall in Maine began on the 24th and lasted nearly four days, finally ending on the 27th. The significance of the storm comes from the exceptionally high snowfall amounts produced across a large part of the state (Fig. 13.2).

On February 22, a small storm developed in the western part of the Gulf of Mexico. Over the next two days, the storm moved up the eastern seaboard, strengthening only slightly. By mid-day on the 24th, snow had spread into Maine. Early on the 25th the storm moved to a position off Cape Cod, with some additional strengthening. From this point until the 28th, the storm meandered off Cape Cod, with only a small amount of additional strengthening. In fact, the storm never reached a high level of intensity— it was only classified as a Category 2 storm on the 1–5 scale developed by Zielinski (2002). The high snowfall totals were a function of the storm's lack of movement, which resulted in a long period of moisture flow off the ocean. This is an excellent example of how a storm of only moderate intensity can have a tremendous impact on a region because of its slow movement.

The impact of the 100-hour storm was especially felt in Maine. In general, more than half the state received at least 20 inches of snow—the only areas not receiving that amount were north of Millinocket (Fig. 13.2). Snow totals fell off dramatically from that point northward. Caribou only received 0.4 inch. Even more impressive is the fact that about one-third of the state, extending from the western mountains eastward through

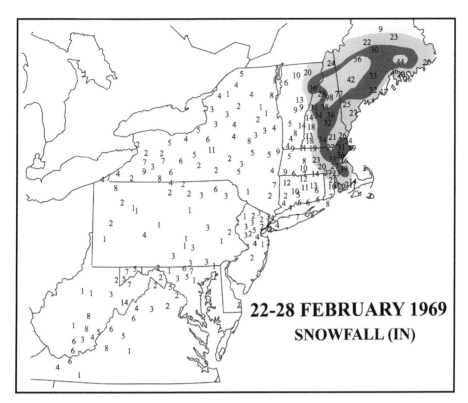

Figure 13.2. Snowfall totals associated with the 100-hour storm of February 22–28, 1969. Figure from Kocin and Uccellinni (2004b, Figure 10.13-1, p. 460) and used with permission from the American Meteorological Society.

the central regions, received more than 30 inches of snow. The ultimate winners from this storm were the western mountains and a small area in the Penobscot River valley. Several areas of the western mountains accumulated 40 inches or more, with 56 inches recorded at Long Falls Dam, 43 in Farmington, and 40 in Rumford. Old Town received 44 inches from the storm, Orono, 41, and Bangor recorded almost 31 inches over the four-day period. More southerly sites also received impressive amounts, with Rockport recording 39 inches, Lewiston more than 36, and Portland, 26.9 inches. Although other blizzards have been known to drop more than 20 inches of snow in parts of the state, there was no storm over the last 200 years that produced such high snowfall totals over such a large part of Maine.

EVENT 3 ■ RAINSTORM OF OCTOBER 1996

The single biggest rainstorm since record keeping began certainly deserves a high rating in the list of top Maine weather events. The meteorological conditions that led to the

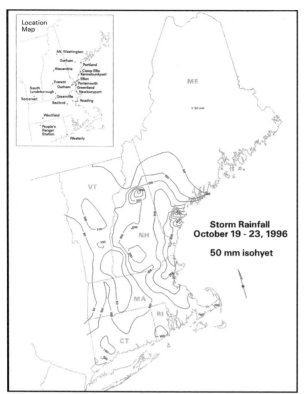

Figure 13.3. Rainfall totals associated with storm of October 1996. The close concentration of lines in the southern coast area of Maine indicates the intensity of the rainfall in that area. Figure from Keim (1998, Fig.2, p. 1063), used with permission from the American Meteorological Society.

tremendous rains of October 19–23, 1996 were simple enough and, like the 100-hour snowstorm, the storm's lack of movement played a key role in its impact on Maine.

There were two major factors that led to the high amounts of rain in southern and coastal Maine. The first was the development of a cut-off low at upper levels (see Ch. 3) of the atmosphere that eventually moved over the Mid-Atlantic states by October 19. It took this cut-off low four days (19th until the 23rd) to move from eastern Pennsylvania to northern Maine. At the same time, a surface low that formed in Colorado moved to Pennsylvania on the 20th where it became occluded. The occluded front also drifted slowly across New England, with low-pressure intensification off the coast on October 21. At the same time, moisture from Hurricane Lili, located about 850 miles southeast of Cape Cod, was pulled into the low-pressure system intensifying off the coast. Ultimately, the combination of the slow-moving upper-level low and the intensifying surface low off the coast, and its associated frontal system, led to 2 to 3 days of hard rain in eastern New England, with the heaviest rain centered on southern Maine (Fig. 13.3).

The record-setting rain measurements were all recorded in Cumberland County, in southern Maine. New records were set for the greatest one-day total for the state—11.74

inches of rain recorded in Portland at the Portland International Jetport on October 21, 1996 (Fig. 13.4)—and the greatest total amount from a single storm—19.3 inches recorded at both Camp Ellis and Gorham (Fig. 13.3). The one-day record superseded the previous record of 8.05 inches from Hurricane Edna recorded in Brunswick on September 11, 1954. To place the 11.74 inches into perspective, this one-day total is just over 25% of the 1971–2000 average annual precipitation for Portland. The storm total of 19.3 inches not only is the existing single greatest precipitation event in Maine, but it also comes in second as the greatest single storm total recorded in New England—first is the 25+ inches dumped on Westfield, Massachusetts, in August 1955 from Hurricane Diane. The 11.74-inch one-day-total recorded in Portland also comes in second in New England for the highest single-day rain total—behind the 18.15 inches that fell in Westfield, Massachusetts, on August 18, 1955.

Adding to the significance of these rainfall totals is the likelihood of an event of this magnitude occurring again. The idea of how often a weather event will occur is the recurrence interval, and one interval most often looked at, especially in preparation for potential flooding, is 100 years. The 100-year recurrence interval means that a storm of a given size is likely to occur only once every 100 years. I should note, however, that this is only a statistical measure. It is conceivable that a storm like the October '96 rainstorm could occur in successive years. In the case of the 1996 rains, according to a study done by Keim (1998), the one-day total of 11.74 inches of rain in Portland nearly doubled former estimates of the 1-day 100-year storm. This also held true for the 19.3-inch storm total. In fact, the total amount received puts this storm as a 400-year event or greater, meaning the statistical likelihood is that Maine will not see such an event again for about 400 years. This was truly a once-in-a-lifetime storm.

EVENT 4 ▨ ALL HALLOWS EVE STORM, OCTOBER 1991

The All Hallows Eve Storm of October 1991 may be one of the most famous of Maine weather events, not so much for what happened in Maine, but because of its overall impact along the eastern seaboard and Sebastian Junger's best-selling book, *The Perfect Storm*, which chronicled the loss of the fishing boat *Andrea Gail*. This is not to say that it was only a minor event in Maine, for it did have a significant impact on the state. It was also interesting from a scientific perspective, given the many factors and uncommon sequence of events that ultimately led to the formation of the storm.

There were three critical factors in the formation of this storm, which helps explain why it has been called the perfect storm. It was, indeed, a rare set of circumstances that ultimately led to the formation of this monster storm. The initial component was a low-pressure system that moved across the United States from Oklahoma into the Northeast on October 26–28, 1991. On the 28th the storm began to reform and intensify as it moved to a position near Sable Island in the Atlantic Ocean south of Newfoundland. The second component that went into the mix was the formation of Hurricane Grace on Sunday, October 27. Hurricane Grace was not a strong hurricane, but it was quite large as it meandered around Bermuda on the 27th and 28th. The third player in the game was

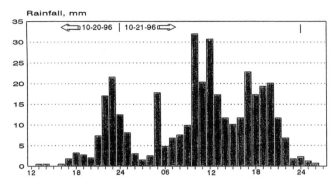

Figure 13.4. Hourly rainfall totals for Portland on October 21, 1996. The 25 mm level is roughly equivalent to 1 inch of rain. Figure from Keim (1998, Figure 3, p. 1064) and used with permission from the American Meteorological Society.

a very strong high-pressure system (1045 mb) east of Hudson Bay that helped generate a strong pressure gradient in the region between this high and the intensifying low-pressure system off Sable Island.

The stage was set by late on the 28th for the formation of a major weather event that would impact not only on Maine, but also the entire east coast of the United States. The first step in the overall sequence of events occurred on the 29th as the energy and moisture of Hurricane Grace became absorbed into the extra-tropical low south of Newfoundland. By October 30, the low, located about 340 nautical miles south of Halifax, Nova Scotia, began to intensify significantly and move to the southwest. The southwest movement, or what is often referred to as retrograding because the dominant movement of storms in the mid-latitudes is west to east, was the second step in the sequence. At this time, ships reported winds of 50–60 knots near the storm and weather buoys in the region reported wave heights of 39 feet. On Halloween, the storm had retrograded to a position west of the North Carolina coast. At the same time the high-pressure system located east of Hudson Bay remained very strong and moved east of Maine off the Newfoundland coast. The high to the north and "The Perfect Storm" to the south produced very strong onshore winds and waves along much of the New England and mid-Atlantic coasts. By November 1, the storm continued to migrate to the southwest, eventually moving over the warm waters of the Gulf Stream. At midday on the 1st, the characteristics of the extra-tropical storm began to change to those of a tropical system, including the formation of an eye. Late in the day on the 1st, the storm had officially become a hurricane. To avoid confusion, it was not officially named by the National Hurricane Center like other hurricanes, but is was referred to as the "Unnamed Hurricane" of 1991. The storm moved back to the northeast, eventually coming ashore in Nova Scotia as a tropical storm. This uncommon weather event wreaked havoc along the coast of Maine and other states on the eastern seaboard.

The storm's impact in Maine was primarily confined to coastal regions in the form of significant wave damage and erosion. Monetary damages in the state were estimated to be about $7.9 million, primarily in Cumberland, Lincoln, Knox, Sagadahoc, and York

Counties, all of which were declared federal disaster counties. Tides along the coastlines of these counties were some 3.4 feet above normal high tide, with wave heights of 15–30 feet. There was severe damage to at least 49 homes, with 2 destroyed. Several lighthouses were damaged, as was President Bush's family compound at Walker Point in Kennebunkport. Significant flooding with the high tides contributed to the damage. High winds knocked down telephone poles and lines and, at sea, many lobster traps were lost. Although total damage was greater in Massachusetts and on the New York and New Jersey coasts, the damage in Maine and the interesting set of meteorological circumstances that caused it, make the All Hallows Eve Storm or "The Perfect Storm" one of Maine's top weather events over the last 200 years.

EVENT 5 ▦ DROUGHT OF 2001

2001 set a record for low precipitation totals—the statewide average was the lowest since 1895. The annual average for the state was only 29.61 inches in 2001—69% of the average annual precipitation of 42.86 inches for the state. It also was 1.37 inches lower than the 30.98 inches received in 1965, the previous lowest average annual precipitation total for the state. The Palmer Drought Severity Index (PDSI)—used to assess the degree of drought or wet conditions—reached a value of -5 by December 2001, the lowest monthly value recorded for the state since 1895 (Fig. 13.5).

The first three months of 2001 were close to average as far as total precipitation amounts and, in fact, the state was coming out of a very snowy winter. Snowfall amounts for that winter were generally much above average, with snow packs easily reaching 3- to 4-foot depths by April 1, 2001. The high snow pack was a result of a snowy winter com-

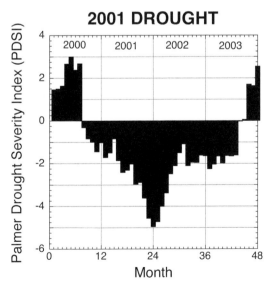

Figure 13.5. This graph of average Palmer Drought Severity Index values for Maine for 2000 through 2003 highlights the severity of the 2001 drought.

Figure 13.6. Low water levels in Ambajejus Lake (left; photo from Catherine Schmitt), and in the St. John (middle) and Piscataquis (right) Rivers during the drought of 2001. Photographs of the St. John and Piscataquis Rivers available from Lombard, 2004.

bined with the lack of a substantial period of thaw during the winter. In addition, four nor'easters hit the state in March 2001, adding significantly to the already substantial snow cover. The water content within the snow pack was quite high, causing many state agencies early in April of 2001 to be concerned with potentially heavy flooding that could occur with the melt, especially if there were a very quick warm spell or a significant rain event. But April 2001 only received an average of 0.94 inch of precipitation, the beginning of the "Drought of 2001."

Only three months that year recorded precipitation values that were above average and two of those were barely above average. March was by the far the wettest month of the year, with 0.43 inch above average, thanks to the four nor'easters that came through the region. June and September were the other two months with above-average precipitation, but June was only 0.10 inches and September a mere 0.01 inch above average. January, April, and August were all at least two inches below average, with April being the driest. The 0.94 inch during April was 2.44 inches below average. All the other months were at least 1.5 inches below average, except February (0.2 inch below average) and July (0.01 inch below average).

Many groundwater monitoring wells and stream gauges of the U. S. Geological Survey recorded record lows from the drought. It has been estimated that 17,000 private wells (roughly 7% of all private wells) around the state went dry sometime during the drought (Lombard, 2004). In addition, at least 35 public water supplies, including eight large community systems, were greatly affected. Most reservoirs around the state had to release water despite having water levels below regulatory minimum flows. All of this led to minimal irrigation capability and the eventual loss of more than $32 million in crops. Some wild blueberry farmers recorded crop losses of 80 to 100%. Many lake and stream levels were well below normal (Fig. 13.6).

In the first few months of 2002, precipitation amounts were closer to normal,

ending the severest part of the 2001 drought. Although meteorological drought conditions were coming to an end early in 2002, hydrological drought conditions persisted in parts of the state for almost the entire year. In fact, 2001 was part of an overall dry period in the early 2000s. During the spring of 2002 there was enough snow pack and total precipitation that streams were flowing close to normal, puddles existed in many yards, and the grass was green—a far cry from the summer and fall of 2001. So, many people were understandably skeptical when the media were still discussing drought. Many water systems, however, especially groundwater systems, are slow to respond to changes in precipitation (see Chapter 6 for a more in-depth discussion about the types of drought). Although the spring of 2002 was close to average in precipitation, it was not nearly enough to replenish groundwater systems to average levels. Parts of Maine remained under hydrological drought conditions through 2002 and into much of 2003. The great impact on the people of Maine in addition to the record-setting precipitation amounts justify picking the drought of 2001 as a top five weather event.

EVENT 6 ▪ HOT SATURDAY, AUGUST 1975

Cold temperatures throughout much of the year and the possibility of snow in some parts of the state nearly any time between September and May are what make many people from away believe that Maine means winter. Consequently, when the state is in the grip of an exceptionally hot spell, it is noteworthy. Even more noteworthy is when the heat also occurs in coastal areas because the sea breeze fails to form. This was the case on Saturday, August 2, 1975. The "Hot Saturday" that effected Maine that day also tortured the rest of New England.

During the last week of July, a large high-pressure system began to move into the eastern U. S. Temperatures remained just above average in most central parts of the state. In the southern part of the state, however, the heat began to build and temperatures reached the 90s. On August 1 the heat spread across the entire state—even in The County temperatures soared into the 90s. By the 2nd, temperatures had reached record levels across most of the state, including coastal areas. The source of the heat was not

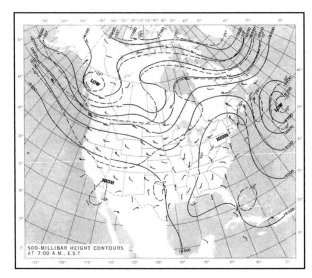

Figure 13.7. Patterns at the 500 mb level on August 2, 1975, showing the strong flow originating south to southwest of Maine with movement around the upper-level high toward Maine and the rest of New England.

only the south to southwesterly flow at the surface, but also a strong upper-level flow from the same areas (Fig. 13.7). Thus, there was a hot flow toward Maine at all levels of the atmosphere, a good reason why the sea breeze never kicked in. Temperatures even reached 90°F in Eastport, a very rare occurrence. The 104°F temperature at Brunswick is the second highest ever recorded.

For most of the state, temperatures dropped somewhat on the 3rd. However, southwestern parts of the state, such as Sanford, suffered through an exceptional 4-day heat wave with three days in a row exceeding 95°F. Following its high of 101°F on the 2nd· Sanford recorded 100°F on the 3rd· Northern areas such as Farmington and Jackman recorded higher temperatures on the 3rd than was recorded on the 2nd—101°F and 97°F, respectively. A backdoor cold front (one that moves into the state from the northeast) finally passed through the state on the 4th, bringing an end to this noteworthy Maine weather event.

EVENT 7 ■ BLIZZARD OF DECEMBER 1962

The unexpected nature of a storm, particularly when the storm ends up being quite large, plays a key role in the storm's notoriety. That is the case for the December blizzard of 1962 that blanketed much of the eastern half of the state with more than 20 inches of snow, including more than three feet in several areas. In fact, 75% of the state received at least 10 inches of snow (Fig. 13.8).

The conditions that led to this major snowstorm were rather simple, but the behavior of the components involved were not that common from a scientific perspective. Those complex details are well beyond any discussion here, so I will only introduce the basic players in the generation of this storm. It was the complexity of the storm and the less sophisticated forecasting of the early 1960s that led forecasters in the Bangor area to miss the eventual magnitude of this storm.

Essentially there were two main features that caused this storm. One was an intensifying low-pressure center located southeast of Cape Cod, mid-day on December 30, 1962 (Fig. 13.8). The second feature was a lengthy stationary front that extended from this low-pressure system north through easternmost Maine. The cold front separated very frigid air moving over Maine on strong northwest winds on its west side from warmer, moist air flowing through the Canadian Maritimes on southeast winds. This contrast in air masses set up the converging air that contributed to the high snowfall totals west of the front. During the rest of the 30th and into the 31st, the low-pressure system moved northwest into the Gulf of Maine, circled into Maine, and then back east again off the coast. This peculiar behavior played a key role in keeping the strong air convergence and snowfall focused on central and eastern Maine. The low-pressure system eventually moved to the northwest by New Years Day, ending a several-day period of intense snowfall in eastern Maine.

Interestingly, the conditions responsible for this storm are nearly identical to those that produced the New England blizzard of March 1888 (Kocin, 1983; Zielinski and Keim, 2003; Kocin and Uccellini, 2004). In that storm, the low-pressure system meandered around Block Island off Rhode Island for several days with a cold front that extended northward through Connecticut, Massachusetts, and New Hampshire. In the case of the Blizzard of 1888, maximum snowfalls were centered west of the front just as in the December 1962 blizzard. The big difference between the two is that the low-pressure center remained stationary for a longer period of time during the 1888 blizzard, thereby producing greater snowfall totals over a more extensive area of western New England

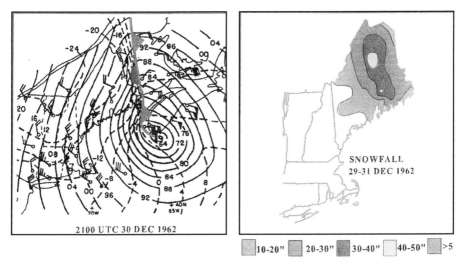

Figure 13.8. Weather map and snowfall amounts associated with the late December blizzard of 1962. Figure from Kocin and Uccellinni (2004a, Figure 6-12, p. 192) and used with permission from the American Meteorological Society.

133

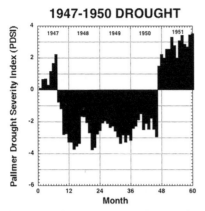

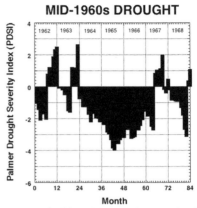

Figure 13.9. Average Palmer Drought Severity Index values for Maine highlight the severity of the 1947 drought (left) and the drought of the mid-1960s (right).

and eastern New York. A greater number of metropolitan areas were also impacted by the Blizzard of 1888. Unfortunately for some people, a storm is only noteworthy when it affects the large metropolitan areas of the eastern United States.

Snowfall totals for the December 1962 storm consistently totaled more than 20 inches across eastern Maine, with more than 10 inches falling through east-central Maine (Fig. 13.8). Augusta received only 9 inches, essentially marking the edge of the 10-inch snowfall line. The most noteworthy snowfall totals may be the 45 inches that fell at Ripogenus Dam, west of Mt. Katahdin and the 25.4 inches that fell in Bangor on the 30th—the greatest snowfall total recorded in Bangor for a single day. This was the only day that the Bangor Daily News failed to publish a paper. Bangor received about 30 inches in all from the storm. Additionally, the storm was a major contributor to the seasonal total of 181.9 inches of snow for Bangor in 1962–63, by far, the city's snowiest winter on record.

EVENT 8 ■ DROUGHTS OF THE LATE 1940S AND MID-1960S
The principle reasons for listing these two events together are that they are the same type of event and were both long lasting. No other event listed here lasted for as long as these two.

Although the drought of the late 1940s did not reach the magnitude of the 2001 drought, nor the longevity of the mid-1960s drought (Figs. 13.5 and 13.9), it is noteworthy for several reasons. One is the particular impact it had on the state. During drought conditions the prevalence of dry timber and grasses results in an increased potential for brush and forest fires. In the late 1940s, peak drought conditions occurred in February of 1948 and again in September of that year, but the record dryness of October 1947 helped produce wildfires that covered much of the eastern half of Mount Desert Island and areas farther south around Kennebunkport. That October marked the start of the drought. The 0.36 inch of precipitation that month make it not only the driest October for Maine, but also the driest month ever recorded. It is only 10% of the total precipitation usually expected during October. In fact, very dry conditions existed from late in 1947 through most of 1950. June, July, and August 1948 made up the driest summer on record, and that September is the driest September on record. While the drought of the late 1940s did not drop water levels to the lows of the 2001 drought, it was nevertheless quite severe.

The fires of October 1947 started slowly on October 17, smoldering for several days. Strong winds on October 21 blew the flames into a raging inferno that engulfed more than 2000 acres. The size of the burned area doubled on the 22nd and the fire remained out of control until October 27. The fire was eventually extinguished by November 14 and the overall damage was mind boggling. Some 200,000 acres burned across the state; 851 permanent homes and 397 seasonal cottages were lost. Perhaps appropriately, 1947 is sometimes referred to as "the year Maine burned."

Prior to 2001, 1965 was the driest year on record for Maine as the average state-wide total for the year was only 30.98 inches of precipitation. The period of drought, however, extended beyond 1965. Drought conditions existed from January 1964 through the spring of 1967 and into 1968 (Fig. 13.9). Water levels around the state may not have reached the record lows recorded in either the late 1940s or the 2001 droughts, but they nevertheless were well below average. This produced 3 or more years of drought across most of the state. The drought also affected most of New England and, in reality, was worse in other states than in Maine. Because Maine is generally thought of as a wet state, these two droughts highlight the potential severity of such events here, and thus, are worthy of being listed together as a top-ten event.

EVENT 9 ■ S.S.*PORTLAND* GALE, NOVEMBER 1898

On November 26, 1898, the Saturday after Thanksgiving, a nor'easter moved into the Gulf of Maine, producing one of the most famous events in the archives of Maine weather. The fame of this storm stems not from of its impact on the state, but from the catastrophic sinking of the S.S. *Portland*, a side-wheel steamship en route from Boston to Portland. As a result, the storm has been coined "The *Portland* Gale."

The Friday after Thanksgiving many people in Boston were returning to Portland after the holiday. The S.S. *Portland* was scheduled to sail to Portland from India Wharf in Boston at 7 PM that evening with 192 passengers and crew. The captain of the ship was Hollis Blanchard, whose actions are at the center of a controversy that has kept the event in the minds of many people in Maine and New England.

Weather forecasts that day clearly stated that a storm was approaching (Fig. 13.10). Initial reports of the impending storm were delivered to the agent for the shipping line by 10:30 that morning. By 3 PM, reports from New York stated that it was snowing there with northeast winds. Nevertheless, Captain Blanchard sailed as scheduled at 7 PM on the evening of November 26. That is where the uncertainty lies. Given the impending storm, many ships did not sail that evening. Why then did the S.S. *Portland*? One explanation put forth is that the owner of the shipping line ordered the boat to sail despite the forecast. Apparently John Liscomb, general manager of the Portland Steam

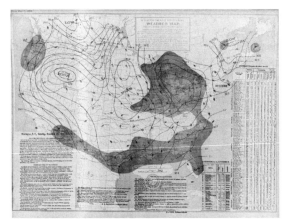

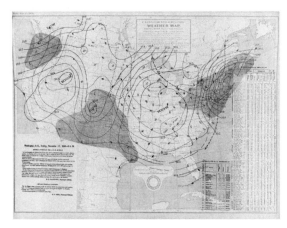

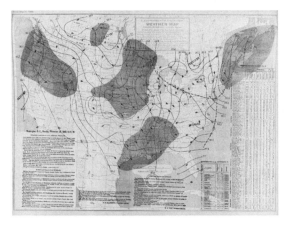

Packet Company, had a reputation for making his boats sail on time, although there were reports that he tried to contact Captain Blanchard about 5:30 in the afternoon suggesting that the ship wait until 9 PM to see how the weather conditions were changing.

A second explanation is that Captain Blanchard sailed despite the warning because he felt he could outrun the storm. At the time he sailed there were just cloudy conditions and the wind direction was thought by some to be indicative of the storm traveling southeast of Boston. There is also speculation that Captain Blanchard wanted to get back to Portland in time for his daughter's birthday party. In Maine, the *Bay State*, sister ship of the *Portland*, was scheduled to leave Portland at 7 PM en route to Boston. Captain Alexander Dennison was told by Liscomb to wait until 9 PM for departure to see how the weather would change. Apparently, Captain Dennison discussed this with Blanchard.

Figure 13.10. Original daily weather maps for 8 AM from November 26 (top), November 27 (middle) and November 28 (bottom), 1898, showing the development of the nor'easter (Portland Gale) that led to the sinking of the S.S. *Portland*.

Reports indicate that Blanchard agreed with the decision since the *Bay State* would be sailing into the storm, but Blanchard felt he could still sail because his path would remain ahead of the storm.

Regardless of the reason for the S.S. *Portland*'s departure, the tragedy began about an hour after they set sail. By that time, the blizzard had overspread the Gulf of Maine. It is believed that the *Portland* was last seen about 9:30 that evening off Cape Ann, Massachusetts. There was no confirmed sighting after that, although four whistle blasts, the international symbol for distress, were heard on Cape Cod at 7 AM on the morning of the 27th. It is uncertain whether or not those blasts came from the *Portland*, but the severity of the weather prevented any rescue from taking place. The exact timing of the sinking is not known, nor is the exact path the ship took. Debris and bodies began washing ashore on Cape Cod late on the 27th. The sighting of a side-wheeler paddle ship in the Gulf of Maine late on the night of the 26th and the distress signal heard early on the morning of the 27th is suggestive of an early-morning end to the *Portland*. Watches on some of the victims had stopped at 9, indicating that the sinking likely occurred at 9 o'clock the morning of the 27th. What is known is that based on sonar investigations across the area, the final resting place of the steamship is on Stellwagen Bank, north of Cape Cod. The loss of 192 lives makes it the most deadly shipwreck in New England waters.

Although the *Portland* sinking is the defining event of the November 26, 1898 nor'easter, it was not the only loss. It is believed that as many as 150 ships were lost in the storm, with an estimated total loss of 450 lives. While the ties the *Portland* had to Maine place this event in the state's top weather events, in fact, the coastal areas hit hardest by the storm were primarily south of Maine, centered on the South Shore of Massachusetts, particularly around Scituate.

EVENT 10 ■ GROUNDHOG DAY STORM, 1976

This very intense nor'easter is notable primarily for the flash flood it caused in the riverfront area of Bangor, but its overall impact extended well beyond that small area. Many coastal areas received very strong winds with flooding, and most of southern and central Maine received more than 1.5 inches of rain. Maine remained on the warm, east side of the storm until it moved well into Canada. Farmington, for instance, received 1.59 inches of precipitation, but only 2 inches of snow on February 3 as the wind came out of the northwest following the storm's exit. Jackman only received 0.54 inch of precipitation and 1.5 inches of snow on the 3rd. Fort Kent received no snow in the 0.85 inch of precipitation recorded there. Higher rainfall totals occurred in central and coastal areas, with Bangor receiving 1.46 inches, Bar Harbor 1.88 inches, Eastport 1.4 inches, Belfast 1.81 inches, and Portland 1.63 inches of precipitation.

The storm formed in the Gulf of Mexico early on February 1 and quickly moved up the east coast. Conditions in the upper atmosphere—such as at the 500 mb level— were ideal for the formation of an intense nor'easter. There was a very deep trough over much of the eastern United States at that level and over the next day it behaved in a classic manner as far as generating conditions perfect for a large nor'easter at the surface. By 1AM on February 2, the surface low-pressure center was located just south of Long Island and winds along the coast were from the northeast at about 10 knots. Three hours later the central pressure had dropped as the storm moved into Connecticut with easterly winds along most of the Maine coast. At 7 AM the pressure had dropped again as the storm moved along the New Hampshire-Maine border. Winds were now primarily from the south at 25 knots or more. The southerly direction was a key ingredient to the notoriety of the storm. The storm continued to strengthen and by 10 AM the center of the storm was located along the northwest Maine-Quebec border. Portland recorded a pressure reading of 959 mb at 10 AM and Bangor dropped out at 955 mb at 11 AM. Winds were still out of the south, with sustained speeds of at least 30 knots. Many areas received higher sustained winds and exceptional gusts. By 1 PM on the 2nd the storm had moved into southern Quebec. Winds had shifted more to the southwest, but they remained strong. Yarmouth, Nova Scotia, recorded sustained winds of 55 knots and offshore buoys southeast of Nova Scotia measured winds of 60 knots. Based on the Zielinski intensity scale, the storm would have been classified as a Category 5 nor'easter.

The strong onshore winds produced tremendous waves and flooding along much of the Maine coast. High tide in most areas came close to noon, adding to the impact. Most places along the coast recorded high tide levels at least 5 feet above normal. Wave heights along the coast reached 14 feet and there was significant coastal flooding. Winds of at least 60 knots were recorded late that morning in Rockland and the U. S. Coast Guard at Southwest Harbor recorded a gust of 100 knots (Morrill, 1977).

The strong southerly winds and timing of high tide were ideal for developing a tremendous tidal surge up the Penobscot River embayment. The surge quickly reached the Kenduskeag Stream in downtown Bangor. Water levels rose almost instantaneously, producing widespread flooding in areas where the Kenduskeag Stream flows into the Penobscot River. The high tide was recorded at 11:30 AM instead of at the predicted time of 12:25 PM and was 10–11 feet above the predicted high tide. This was the highest difference between actual and predicted high tides in the state from the storm. Some areas along the coast had high tides 7–8 feet above predicted levels, but they were probably enhanced by wave action. Water levels in the Kenduskeag Plaza in Bangor rose to a depth of 12 feet in less than 15 minutes. Approximately 200 vehicles were submerged from the rising waters. Several people had to be rescued from the roofs of their vehicles. Estimated damage was more than $2 million, primarily from flooded basements and vaults in downtown banks.

This is the only known tidal surge to produce such flooding in the Bangor area. It took a very rare combination of parameters to produce such an event: a very intense nor'easter, a storm track that produced very strong winds directly up the Penobscot River, and the timing to coincide with high tide.

HONORABLE MENTION

SAXBY'S GALE, OCTOBER 1869: This event may be the most interesting of the events listed here, not so much for its intensity or impact, but for the events that preceded its formation. This storm consisted of two major weather makers, one an advancing cold front, probably associated with an upper-level trough that advanced into Maine, the other a hurricane that apparently came ashore in the Brunswick area. While these two features combined to cause considerable damage throughout much of eastern Maine, the event's notoriety comes more from the fact that the storm was predicted—at least in general— almost a year before it happened.

Stephen Martin Saxby was born in England in 1804, possibly attaining the rank of lieutenant in the British Royal Navy. At the very least, he was a civilian naval engineering instructor, though his exact position is unclear (Rao, 2002). He was very interested in weather prediction, particularly using the cycles of the moon. His fame, or perhaps his infamy, came about as he studied the solar and lunar tables from *The Nautical Almanac* in late 1868. On Christmas Day 1868, Saxby wrote a letter to the London newspaper, *The Standard*, stating that at 7 AM on October 5, 1869, the moon will be at her nearest to the earth. Saxby indicated that this would result in a maximum gravitational pull and that the moon will be over the equator at noon the same day. He also noted that by 2 PM on the 5th, the sun and moon would be in the same arc of ascension, meaning that their gravitational attraction on the earth would be in the same direction. All these factors led Saxby to predict that there would be an atmospheric disturbance on October 5, 1869, ten months after making his prediction. Interestingly, he made no prediction as to where, other than somewhere in the North Atlantic, this disturbance would occur, a point he emphasized in a second letter to the paper in September 1869. The reason he gave for not predicting a location was that his prediction was based on astronomical and tidal considerations, which are global (Rao, 2002).

Although Saxby did not directly predict a storm would hit Maine that October, an interesting series of events probably led to its identification as Saxby's Gale. Frederick Allison wrote a regular monthly column for the *Halifax Evening Express* and in the October 1, 1869 edition, he used Saxby's prediction to focus on the possibility that the disturbance could very well occur in the Canadian Maritimes. Allison stated in his column that a heavy gale would hit the Halifax area on Tuesday, October 5. Apparently, word got around, because many people became very concerned about a large storm hitting the area.

Late in the day on October 3 or very early on the 4th, a hurricane formed east of South Carolina in the Atlantic Ocean and quickly headed northeast on a direct line to eastern Maine and the Maritimes. It was at Category 2 level (83–95 knot or 96–110 mph sustained winds) upon formation and maintained that strength as it moved northeastward and then slightly more northerly by mid-day. The hurricane made landfall around Brunswick by midnight of the 4th still as a Category 2 storm. It dropped to Category 1 after coming ashore, and then to tropical storm level by early in the morning on the 5th as it moved through Aroostook County.

Over this same period, a cold front associated with a strong low-pressure trough was moving across the Hudson River Valley and into New England (Ludlum, 1963). This was a powerful weather-maker in its own right as a very strong, moist southerly flow ahead of the front caused very heavy downpours in the northeast, particularly on the 2nd and 3rd. On the 4th, precipitation and winds increased dramatically as the approaching hurricane contributed energy and precipitation to the frontal system as it moved through New England. Areas in southern New England were more affected by rain than wind, with many places easily receiving more than 6 inches of rain, while Canton, Connecticut, received up to 12.25 inches. Interestingly, the hurricane may have converted into more of an extra-tropical system as it interacted with the front. The nature of wind patterns across Maine on the 4th was not consistent with a distinct tropical system moving through the state.

Regardless of what became of the hurricane as it met the cold front, the heavy rain, strong winds, and remarkably high tide levels caused many fatalities and severe damage, primarily in easternmost Maine and the Canadian Maritimes. Many barns were blown down, chimneys cut off, and vessels pushed onshore in the MDI area, with even greater damage around Eastport. As many as 40 buildings either had their roofs blown off or were destroyed in the region and it is estimated that the towns of Lubec, Pembroke, and Perry had losses of at least $500,000, a significant amount for the late 1800s. The southerly exposure of Passamaquody Bay allowed the wind-driven tides to be carried all the way up the St. Croix River to Calais, and the winds, as well, led to the destruction of many vessels, wharves, fish houses, and stores. It was reported that 67 vessels were grounded in Eastport Harbor, and 17 lives were lost when the schooner *Rio* sank in St. Andrews Bay. Another report from an individual traveling from the Eastport to Calais the day after the storm stated that 90 houses were either blown down or seriously damaged.

New Brunswick, Canada, may have been hit the hardest, with an estimated loss of 100 lives in easternmost areas of the province, including the destruction of about 100 buildings in St. Stephen. The high tides also damaged most of the wharves in St. Andrews.

Had both Saxby's and Allison's predictions come to fruition? Perhaps it is only coincidence that Saxby predicted the event to the day ten months before it occurred. There is certainly little evidence that tidal changes exert enough energy to cause storm formation. Adding the fact that Saxby would not predict where the storm would hit, you'd be hard pressed to say definitively that his prediction was accurate.

WINTER COLD OF 1970–71: For some reason very cold winters do not seem to get recognition as major weather events in Maine. Perhaps it is because we are so used to them that a particularly cold winter blends into so many of the past. The winter of 1970–71, however, stands out as a "particularly" cold winter that deserves mention. For example, from New Years Day to early February 1971, there were 24 days when the low temperature in Bangor dropped below 0°F, and there were only 8 days between January 8 and February 6 when the low was above 0°F. On seven of those days, the low temperature fell below –20°F and on two days, the daily high temperature remained below 0°F. Conditions were equally frigid in Caribou, where there were seven days when the high temperature remained below 0°F.

Even southern coastal parts of the state felt the cold that winter. There were 18 days from January 1 to February 4 when the low temperature in Portland fell below 0°F. Although cold spells are not necessarily rare in Maine, this two-month stretch surely tested the resolve of Mainers. There must have been many frozen pipes that winter.

WINTER SNOWS AND RESULTING FLOODS OF 1987: One of the joys of spring in Maine is finally getting out from under the weight of winter. Longer days and warmer temperatures bring about the thaw. Unfortunately, in the spring of 1987, the thaw was more than we bargained for. That winter had truly been "snowy," with many places easily receiving more than their average snowfall amounts. It was also a cold winter. There were fewer periods of melting, so much of the snow remained on the ground. By the beginning of April there was a very deep snow pack. A large rainstorm on March 31 set the stage for disaster as extensive flooding affected much of northern and central Maine. A rapid rise in the Kennebec River produced flooding in Augusta, and Lowe's Bridge, a 130-year-old covered bridge on the Piscataquis River between Guilford and Sangerville, was washed away. The entire business district in downtown Hallowell was flooded by April 2.

YEAR WITHOUT A SUMMER, 1816: The beginning of the 1810s was a rather chilly period in our history, and it culminated in the infamous "Year Without a Summer." As discussed earlier, the cold weather of 1816 was a result of the eruption of Mt. Tambora, and that year saw a frigid summer throughout much of the eastern United States and Europe. New England was hit particularly hard, as measurable snow was recorded in June as far south as western Massachusetts and frost occurred in parts of New England in July and August. Such weather had a devastating effect on agriculture, ultimately leading to a period of out-migration from Maine.

MAINE HURRICANES: Many hurricanes have impacted the state, but there isn't one in particular that stands out as the most severe or the most destructive. Wayne Cottery (1996; www.pivot.net/~cotterly/history.htm) has summarized many of these storms and to say one was worse than another is difficult. For people along the coast, certain storms simply by their track may have had a greater impact than others. Hurricane Bob in October of 1991 caused significant damage in southern and midcoast areas. It came ashore around Narragansett Bay and the Rhode Island/Massachusetts border before crossing into the Gulf of Maine and coming ashore again in the midcoast region. It was a very destructive storm and caused three fatalities in Maine. It is the most recent significant hurricane to impact the state, but Hurricane Edna, which struck on September 11–12, 1954, could be considered the worst hurricane of the last 200 years as it caused eight fatalities and produced more than 8 inches of rain in Brunswick. Adding to Edna's significance was that Hurricane Carol had passed through New England just a week prior. With wind damage, storm surges that cause coastal flooding, and heavy rainfall that causes stream and street flooding, hurricanes are a triple threat to Maine.

14

WEATHER OF THE PAST

Is Maine's weather changing over time? And, if so, in what ways? That question is much in the news and on the minds of many people, ranging from scientists to farmers, from politicians to people on the street. Certainly there are grave concerns about whether overall weather conditions and our climate are changing, and whether human activity has been a leading cause of these changes. Of particular concern is the issue of global warming and potentially severe socioeconomic repercussions its impact may have on the state. For example, if precipitation amounts change radically, Maine might experience more droughts or stronger, more frequent damaging storms? Changes in snowfall amounts could be very damaging to the skiing industry, as well as to others who enjoy wintertime activities, including snowmobilers. There could be changes in vegetation that result in a weaker fall tourist industry because deciduous trees migrate farther north. And fewer maple trees would also be devastating to the sugaring industry. These are only a few of the ways Maine livelihoods depend on the weather and climate.

The key to determining which aspects of the climate are changing and the magnitude of change is to evaluate data sets that extend as far back in time as possible, with as many records (preferably daily) as possible. Instrumental records provide these data, but they are limited to just over 100 years. Nevertheless, these data allow us to evaluate our changing climate over at least the last century.

In addition to instrumental records, anecdotal evidence of changing conditions can either support or challenge the instrumental records. These anecdotal pieces of evidence include such items as the timing of ice-out on lakes, timing of the high flow of rivers, as well as periodic biological evidence, such as the timing of lilac blooms and the first appearance of certain birds in the spring. Some of these anecdotal data may go farther back in time than the instrumental record, extending the overall length of climatic records.

Changing weather conditions may also be examined in written records as available in diaries, journals, annals, and newspapers. Although these data are often not quantitative, they can provide valuable information on specific weather conditions as far back as the 1600s. Changes in the frequency and magnitude of extreme weather events are particularly available from past written records. Due to the complex nature of our climate it is important to use as many pieces of evidence as possible to determine how our climate is changing and what may happen in the future.

The Question: How has Maine's weather and climate been changing?
Keep in mind that none of these data sets are "perfect," but taken together they can illustrate the possible trends in climate change.

■ MEAN ANNUAL TEMPERATURE

Answer 1: Maine's climate is cooling as a whole, but the cooling is not uniform across the state.

The Data Used: The complete instrumental record from climatic stations across the state beginning in 1895. The mean annual temperature (MAT) for the state is determined by adding the MAT for each climatic division as a proportion of the area of the state covered by each division. Essentially the northern climatic division (Fig. 4.3) is dominant when using this technique because it occupies over 50% of the land area of the state.

The MAT for the state over this time period of 1895 to 2007 is 41.2°F (Fig. 14.1), but there is quite a bit of year-to-year variability. To determine an approximate trend in the state's temperatures over the 100+ years of record, a statistical straight line of the data is shown. Other evaluations may require complex explanations or exceptions, and the straight-line format provides the most straightforward interpretation of data. It gives an idea of what is happening in general to Maine's MAT.

The results indicate that the MAT for Maine has decreased by about 0.27°F since 1895 or about -0.24°F/100 years. However, the linear trend shown barely represents 1% of the variability in the record. For all three climatic divisions, there is a lot of variability in the data. The statewide average is reflected in the trends for the three climatic divisions. The northern division shows a trend that indicates a -0.94°F (-0.84°F/100 years) cooling. The south central division essentially shows no trend, as the linear fit indicates a <0.1°F warming. Essentially this small change suggests that MATs have not changed since 1895. On the other hand, climatic division 3, the coastal zone, displays a warming trend of +1.14°F since 1895 or +1.02°F/100 years. However, the coastal climatic division only represents 15% of the area of the state, so it has little impact on the statewide average.

Interestingly, the overall trends in temperature over the last century seem to follow a 30-year cycle. Generally speaking, temperatures from around 1900 to 1930 averaged below the long-term state average of 41.2°F, the next 30-year period of 1930–60 was

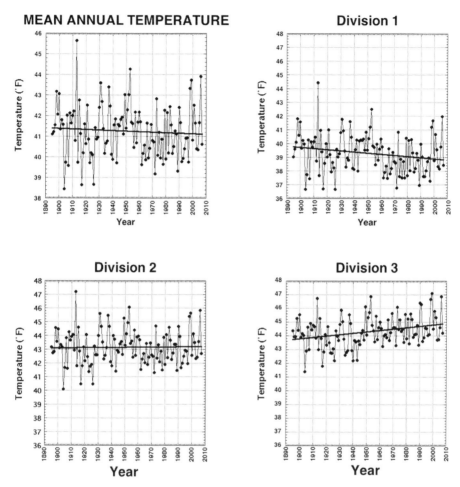

Figure 14.1. Statistical straight line indicating the Mean Annual Temperature (MAT) for the state. Constructed from data from the National Climatic Data Center. The line indicates the best-fit linear trend to the data.

generally below that. More recently, 1960 through around 1990 were much cooler than the long-term average, and the 1990s indicate an overall higher than average MAT, so it will be interesting to see if that trend continues through the 2010s.

The Problems: Two major concerns need to be considered when reviewing the results of this data set. One is the way the climate stations are incorporated. At the time a new station was established, its data were incorporated into the divisional average, and thus the state average. This means that there are periods of time when only a selected number of stations were used to determine averages for larger areas of the state and for each climatic division.

The biggest potential problem with this technique is that most of the recent stations are in northern areas and in the hills of western Maine—the two coldest parts of the state. So the decreasing trend in temperature for the northern climatic division could simply be a function of adding more "cold" stations at a later time in the overall record.

The second concern is the limited number of stations during the early part of the record. There were perhaps only a handful of stations during the first several decades, including those in Portland and Eastport. It was not until around 1926 when more stations were established, such as those in Lewiston and Farmington. More stations were added in the late 1940s, but many not until 1948. So the question is, particularly for the earliest part of the 1900s and the late 1800s, how representative are these records for what really has been happening in Maine over the last century?

The Supporting Elements: There is a viable explanation why northern parts of Maine show a cooling trend compared to the warming trend along the coast. The northern part of the state is often under the influence of a different weather pattern than southern and coastal areas. In particular, there are many times when a low-pressure system remains in place to the northeast of the state and produces a prevalent northwest airflow into northern and sometimes central locations. This would produce cooler conditions overall in those areas. There are also many times when a weather system will affect coastal and

Table 14.1. Top Ten Hottest and Coldest Years (Average Annual Temperature) for the State of Maine, 1895–2007, sorted according to temperature.

	Hottest Years with Annual Temperature		Difference from Average	Percentage of Average	Coldest Years with Annual Temperature		Difference from Average	Percentage of Average
1	1913	45.7°F	+4.5°F	111%	1904	38.4°F	-2.8°F	93%
2	1953	44.3°F	+3.1°F	107%	1917	38.6°F	-2.6°F	94%
3	2006	43.9°F	+2.7°F	107%	1926	38.7°F	-2.5°F	94%
4	1999	43.7°F	+2.5°F	106%	1972	39.2°F	-2.0°F	95%
5	1931	43.6°F	+2.4°F	106%	1989	39.3°F	-1.9°F	95%
6	1937	43.4°F	+2.2°F	105%	1907	39.6°F	-1.6°F	96%
7	1998	43.3°F	+2.1°F	105%	1962	39.6°F	-1.6°F	96%
8	1898	43.2°F	+2.0°F	105%	1978	39.7°F	-1.5°F	96%
9	1900	43.1°F	+1.9°F	105%	1943	39.7°F	-1.5°F	96%
10	1952	43.0°F	+1.8°F	104%	1923	39.7°F	-1.5°F	96%
11	1949	43.0°F	+1.8°F	104%	1905	39.7°F	-1.5°F	96%
12					1914	39.7°F	-1.5°F	96%

Note: Average annual temperature for 1895–2007 is 41.2°F....

Table 14.2. Record Monthly and Seasonal Average Temperature, 1895–2007 for the State of Maine.

	Maximum (°F)	Year	Difference from Average (%)	Minimum (°F)	Year	Difference from Average (%)	Long-Term Average (°F)
Monthly							
January	24.8	1913	+10.2 (170%)	4.1	1994	-10.5 (28%)	14.6
February	27.4	1981	+9.1 (168%)	6.3	1934	-10.0 (39%)	16.3
March	35.4	1946	+8.6 (132%)	18.7	1923	-8.1 (70%)	26.8
April	44.5	1910	+5.3 (113%)	33.2	1926	-6.0 (85%)	39.2
May	57.6	1911	+6.5 (113%)	44.3	1967	-6.8 (87%	51.1
June	66.1	1930	+5.4 (109%)	55.9	1958	-4.8 (92%)	60.7
July	71.4	1952	+5.1 (108%)	61.3	1962, 1992	-5.0 (92%)	66.3
August	70.1	1937	+5.8 (109%)	59.1	1964	-5.2 (92%)	64.3
September	62.7	1961	+6.5 (112%)	51.7	1978	-4.5 (92%	56.2
October	57.7	1913	+12.2 (127%)	38.5	1925	-7.0 (85%)	45.5
November	39.4	1931	+5.8 (117%)	26.6	1933	-7.0 (79%)	33.6
December	29.4	1900	+9.0 (144%)	5.3	1989	-15.1 (26%)	20.4
Seasonal							
Winter	23.5	1933	+6.4 (137%)	9.8	1918	-7.3 (57%)	17.1
Spring	43.5	1921	+9.8 (111%)	33.7	1926, 1967	-5.3 (86%)	39.0
Summer	67.1	1937	+3.3 (105%)	60.4	1903	-3.4 (95%)	63.8
Fall	50.9	1913	+5.8 (113%)	41.6	1904	-3.5 (92%)	45.1

southern parts, but not central and northern parts of the state. In fact, overall trends in Maine differ from those in other parts of New England because of this influence of different circulation systems in northern Maine than in the rest of the region. For example, the fourth coldest year on record for Maine was 1972 (Table 14.1), but this year does not show up among the top five coldest years in any other New England state.

Apparently, temperatures seem to move in general 30-year cycles. The existing record looks at two periods of generally cooler than average temperature, and only one period of warmer than average temperature. Taken as a whole, the three cycles would indicate an overall cooling trend when looked at from a linear perspective. This aspect brings out the importance of the length of records when the climate may have a cyclical

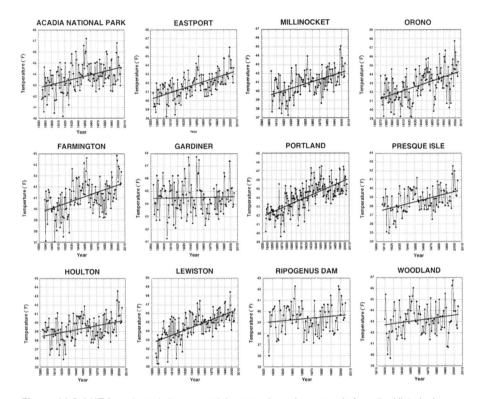

Figure 14.2. MAT for selected sites around the state, based on records from the Historical Climatology Network (HCN). Data have been adjusted for any urbanization. Graphs constructed from data from the National Climatic Data Center. Solid lines indicate the best-fit linear trends to the data.

nature to it, as appears to be the case for MAT in Maine. Only the next few decades will show whether or not this general cycle remains intact.

Answer 2: Maine's climate is warming across the state.

The Data Used: The Historical Climate Network (HCN) data set consists of 12 stations in Maine whose records have been adjusted for moves of station, urbanization, and observation times. The length of record varies for each station. See Table 4.2 for a list of the stations in Maine that comprise the HCN.

The Findings: The temperature trends depicted by this data set indicate that Maine has been warming, especially since the 1930s. The advantage the HCN data set has over the combined records of every station in the state is the statistical adjustments made to the HCN records to account for urbanization, variable timing of observations, and station moves; these all have the potential to bias the records. The time period covered by most stations is the same, although some span different time frames (Table 14.2). Nevertheless, the consistency from station to station for the period covered, as well as the consistency within each station's record, make these numbers more reliable when determining long-term trends.

Linear trends in the data for all 12 stations indicate that MAT has been warming since the late 1800s and early 1900s (Fig. 14.2; Table 14.1). Seven of the twelve stations show an increase of more than 2°F per 100 years, while three stations (Acadia National Park, Houlton, and Woodland) indicate an increase between 1 and 1.5°F/100 years. Only two sites (Gardiner and Ripogenus Dam) show and increase of <1°F/100 years. There is no trend in any part of the state that indicates consistent temperature increases. In addition, there are only two years prior to 1930 that fall into the hottest years on record, but seven years prior to 1930 that fall into the top ten coldest years (Table 14.1).

The Problems: Although the consistency of the HCN stations makes for more reliable data, the major problem is the small number of stations that are used. There are more than 200 stations in the network, yet only 12 have been adjusted for potential problems. The difficulty is determining whether these 12 stations are actually representative of statewide trends in temperature change. Roughly half the state, primarily the northern to northwestern parts, is represented by only a few stations (Presque Isle, Houlton, and Ripogenus Dam). Finally, not all of these HCN stations are in ideal locations. For example, the Orono station is located on the roof of the physics building on the UMaine campus, where the blacktop roof absorbs heat and can produce artificially high numbers.

■ SEASONAL TEMPERATURE TRENDS

Answer 1: The greatest decreases in temperature occur in the transitional seasons of fall and spring, with winters showing a slight increase in temperature.

The Data: Evaluation of seasonal temperature trends are presented using the months typically representative of the solar seasons: winter (December, January, February), Spring (March, April, May), summer (June, July, August) and fall (September, October, November). The data set used is the complete record from Maine stations since 1895.

Winter: The statewide average for each season of the year is presented in Figure 14.3. Given the decreasing trend in temperature for mean annual temperature, it is not surprising that two of the four seasons show a decrease in temperature with time. One is spring, which shows a decrease of 0.4°F. The fall also shows a decrease, but a much more significant one of 1.03°F since 1895. Summer temperatures statewide show no trend, but the winter shows a temperature increase since 1895 of 0.26°F. The linear trend for each season represents less than 3% of the data.

The Problems: The primary problem with these trends is the same as with the mean annual temperature trends for the entire state. Including the data from stations that have been added to the network over time may skew the resulting trends.

The Supporting Thoughts: The trend for winter temperatures in this data set may well be true. Many environmental changes support the likelihood that winter temperatures have been warmer in recent years. Many long-time residents also point out that the winters just don't seem to be as cold or snowy as they were 30–40 years ago.

■ PRECIPITATION TRENDS

Answer 1: Maine's climate has been getting drier.

The Data: As with mean annual temperature, the complete instrumental record from climate stations across the state beginning in 1895 is also used to determine mean annual precipitation (MAP). Data are evaluated for the entire state and for each climatic division established by the National Climatic Data Center (NCDC). Annual precipitation for the state is determined by adding the levels for each climatic division as a proportion of the area of the state covered by each division. Again, as with temperature, the northern climatic division (Fig. 4.3) is essentially dominant simply because it occupies more than 50% of the land area of the state.

The Findings: The general statewide trend shows a decrease of about 6.00 inches, or 14.1%, of the long-term average of 42.86 inches (Fig. 14.4). Most of that decrease occurred from the late 1800s until around 1950. Since 1950, the linear trend indicates a decrease of only 0.39 inch for the state. One reason for the greater decrease earlier in the record is the very wet part of the early 1900s, as the three years of 1900–02 are among the six wettest years (Table 14.3). Trends for the climatic divisions differ much as they do for temperature; Divisions 1 and 2 reveal a similar pattern and Division 3 (the coast) shows an opposite, that is, wetter trend. Division 1 shows a decrease of 6.8 inches (6.07 in/100 years), while Division 2 shows a decrease of 2.64 inches (2.36 in/100 years). Division 3 shows an increase of 2.92 inches (2.61 in/100 years).

The Problems: Using precipitation data from all the climate stations in Maine to determine statewide trends has the same potential problems as for determining temperature trends. The data set incorporates each station as it becomes active, so there is no consistency in the number of stations used over the 100-plus years of record. Similarly, if a station becomes inactive, the data from that station essentially drops from the calculations for that division. Furthermore, the number of stations for the earliest part of the record is quite small, and most of those are located in southern and coastal areas—the generally wetter parts of the state.

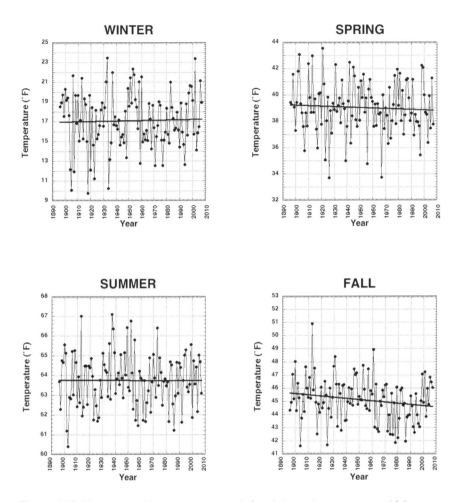

Figure 14.3. Mean state wide temperature trends for winter, spring, summer, and fall, as constructed from data from the National Climatic Data Center. Solid lines indicate the best-fit linear trends to the data.

The Supporting Thoughts: The reliability of the precipitation trends in the three climatic divisions may be supported if there has been a slight east-to-southeast shift of the major storm tracks over time. The same result could also be produced with a change in the frequency of storms, particularly coastal storms, with time. An eastward shift in the storm track would easily increase coastal precipitation, but would cause a decrease in the two inland divisions, with the greatest decrease occurring in the northern part of the state. These possibilities take into account potential changes in extra-tropical storm systems, but do not consider changes in tropical system numbers or tracks. Tropical systems are, in fact, major precipitation producers for the state, and years when a large tropical

Table 14.3. Top Ten Wettest and Driest Years for the State of Maine, 1895–2007

	Wettest Years with Annual Precipitation		Difference from Average	Percentage of Average	Driest Years with Annual Precipitation		Difference from Average	Percentage of Average
1	2005	61.12 in.	+18.26 in.	143%	2001	29.61 in.	-13.25 in.	69%
2	1900	58.35 in.	+15.93 in.	136%	1965	30.98 in.	-11.88 in.	72%
3	1954	56.40 in.	+13.98 in.	132%	1941	32.19 in.	-10.67 in.	75%
4	1920	56.21 in.	+13.79 in.	131%	1985	33.54 in.	-9.32 in.	78%
5	1983	54.19 in.	+11.77 in.	126%	1955	33.92 in.	-8.94 in.	79%
6	1901	54.08 in.	+11.66 in.	126%	1957	34.28 in.	-8.58 in.	80%
7	1902	53.91 in.	+11.49 in.	126%	964	34.29 in.	-8.57 in.	80%
8	1973	51.41 in.	+8.99 in.	120%	1978	34.51 in.	-8.35 in.	80%
9	1898	51.35 in.	+8.93 in.	120%	1980	35.63 in.	-7.23 in.	83%
10	1897	51.11 in.	+8.69 in.	119%	1949	35.75 in.	-7.11 in.	83%

Note: Average annual precipitation for 1895-2007 is 42.86 inches

system affects the state tend to have greater total precipitation amounts, especially along the coast. The high tropical activity in the 1950s and then again in the '90s may have contributed to the overall trend of increasing precipitation in coastal areas.

■ SEASONAL PRECIPITATION TRENDS

Answer 1: The fall has been getting wetter in Maine.

The Data: Using the complete Maine data set of stations, all the seasons except fall show the same general decrease over time as the statewide average. Winter trends show a decrease of 3.17 inches, or 31.8% of the long-term average of 9.97 inches. Most of that decrease occurred from 1895 to 1930. Since then, there appears to be a roughly 20-year cycle in winter precipitation with very little linear trend. Spring shows less of a decrease in precipitation of 1.78 inches, or 16.9% of the 10.53-inch average. This is similar to the winter trend, as springs were much wetter until about 1930. Since then, they have been more erratic with no indication of a cyclical behavior. Summer precipitation appears to have decreased by 0.92 inch or 8.3% of the 11.07-inch average. There is no distinct trend for summer in earlier parts of the record, as with winter and spring. The only distinct period is the late 1910s and earliest 1920s when three of the four wettest summers over the entire record occurred. Fall precipitation, on the other hand, appears to have increased by 1.39 inches (1.24 in/100 years), or 12.3% of the average of 11.30 inches. The most noticeable change is in the very wet falls within the last 9 years, including 2005, the wettest fall on record by far, and 1999, the third wettest on record.

The Overall Answer

Coming to grips with an overall answer to how Maine's weather has been changing may be as tough as it is to predict the weather in a 3-day forecast. The biggest difficulty is that we just do not have completely adequate and reliable records of climate change over the last 100 years. Unfortunately, you can almost always get the answer you want by looking at one of the particular data sets, and not the others, which leads to a true dilemma in trying to predict what might happen in the future. However, it is important to realize that Maine's weather is quite complex and does not necessarily follow the weather and climate trends of other parts of the New England, or the world as a whole.

Pre-instrumental Period

In addition to the recorded changes of the last 100 years, there is a wealth of information available on prior weather conditions. It comes from the written records kept by indi-

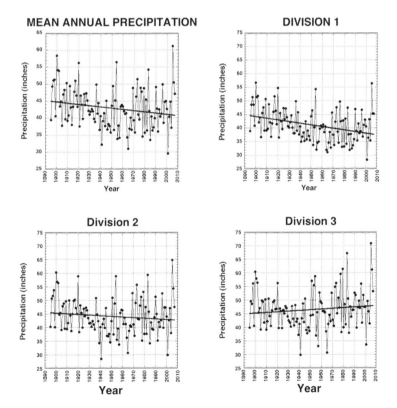

Figure 14.4. Mean annual precipitation (MAP) for the state and for the three climatic divisions of the state as constructed from data from the National Climatic Data Center. The solid line indicates the best-fit linear trend to the data.

Table 14.4. Record Monthly and Seasonal Precipitation, 1895–2007

	Maximum (inches)	Year	Difference from Average (%)	Minimum (inches)	Year	Difference from Average (%)	Long-Term Average (inches)
Monthly							
January	7.80	1979	+4.40 (229%)	0.59	1970	-2.81 (17%)	3.40
February	8.63	1900	+5.69 (293%)	0.47	1987	-2.47 (16%)	2.94
March	10.83	1902	+7.19 (297%)	0.43	1915	-3.21 (12%)	3.64
April	7.34	1901	+3.96 (217%)	0.81	1966	-2.57 (24%)	3.38
May	7.16	1984	+3.65 (204%)	0.77	1903	-2.74 (22%)	3.51
June	10.50	1917	+6.83 (286%)	1.23	1913	-2.44 (33%)	3.67
July	7.40	1915	+3.77 (204%)	1.11	1952	-2.52 (31%)	3.63
August	8.17	1991	+4.40 (217%)	1.08	2002	-2.69 (29%)	3.77
September	9.10	1999	+5.41 (247%)	1.26	1948	-2.43 (34%)	3.69
October	11.39	2005	+4.11 (318%)	0.36	1947	-3.22 (10%)	3.58
November	9.57	1983	+5.53 (237%)	0.74	1939	-3.30 (18%)	4.04
December	8.76	1973	+5.13 (241%)	0.94	1943	-2.69 (26%)	3.63
Seasonal							
Winter	19.46	1898	+9.49 (195%)	4.60	1944	-5.37 (46%)	9.97
Spring	18.53	19.01	+8.00 (176%)	4.60	1965	-5.93 (44%)	10.53
Summer	20.99	1917	+9.92 (190%)	7.49	1948	-3.58 (68%)	11.07
Fall	22.21	2005	+10.90 (196%)	6.30	1984	-5.01 (56%)	11.31

viduals through their diaries, journals, and annals, as well as through newspaper articles. The use of written records to reconstruct past conditions is called historical climatology. Here in Maine, written records extend back into the 1600s, when Europeans first came to the region. As a result, it is possible to evaluate how weather conditions have changed over roughly the last 300 to 400 years. Most of these written records cover the 1800s and later parts of the 1700s, but there are still enough records prior to that to at least get a feeling for weather conditions in the earlier parts of the 1700s and the 1600s.

The information from these records is often more qualitative than quantitative. For example, many written records, such as personal diaries, give accounts of temperature using such terms as very cold, cool, warm, hot—reflecting the subjective thoughts of the diarist. But if there are enough records available for a given part of the state, you can get a good idea of overall temperature conditions at the time. Similarly, precipitation events are recorded using terms like rain, drizzle, thunderstorms, snow, and hail. When temperature and precipitation type are recorded, together with wind directions and sky conditions, you can determine fairly well where low- and high-pressure systems and their associated fronts were situated.

A couple of examples give an indication of weather conditions during several years in the late 1700s. The Longfellow diary of South Gorham indicated that the spring of 1779 was quite cold. The records indicate that temperatures for March 15–20 were "cold like weather in January." On March 22 temperatures remained cold with a northeast snowstorm that produced 3.5 inches of snow, as recorded by Longfellow in the March 23 entry. December of 1799 appears to have been quite cold, according to Caleb Bradley of Portland. He has several accounts of very cold conditions (4th, 9th, and 17–18th) as well as several entries of cold days, as on the 5th, 10th, 13th, 19th, and Christmas Eve. Undoubtedly Portland had a white Christmas that year; Bradley recorded snowfall on the 6th, 8th, 17th, 21st, and 23rd. And in Freeport, according to the diary of John Cushing, 16 inches of snow fell that year from November 29 to December 4.

The types of weather that seem to have received the most attention in past accounts are, logically, big storms or significant weather events. Just as we see today when large storms and their impact dominate the media, significant weather events were often highlighted in personal accounts. Weather plays a tremendous role in our life today, as it always has in the lives of Mainers.

There are many ideal examples of past severe snowstorms. One is the Long Storm of November 18–22, 1798, when Jeremiah Weare, Jr. of York recorded nearly 3 feet of snow over a 5-day period. On March 10, 1819, Professor Cleaveland of Bowdoin College recorded 30 inches, 10 inches more than the next largest snow recorded during the period from 1807 to 1859. A large storm dumped 20 inches on East Machias on October 29, 1793, as was taken from notes of John Peters, (Ludlum, 1976). Peters also noted, "Snow north of East Machias 20 inches on level and fairly up to the waist band of my Breeches in Swamps. I don't think the oldest man on earth ever saw such a snow the first that came." As of November 1, he noted "The snow is so thick on the trees and so very deep on the ground, that we can do nothing at present." An example of an early season storm comes from J. W. Hanson of Gardiner, who noted that the "Snow in October 1793 covered potatoes in the field." Likewise, on November 18, 1873, a severe nor'easter, whose pressure was measured as 964 mb in Portland produced 64-mph winds in Eastport, heavy snow inland, and rain in coastal regions. This storm was much like the strong nor'easter that hit coastal areas on December 7, 1869. A late season storm on March 31–April 1, 1807 dropped 20 inches of wet snow in Gardiner. In addition, there have been winter seasons that produced much more snow than has been observed recently. For instance the winter of 1748 is characterized by many snowstorms and a lack of significant melting. The Rev. T. Smith from Portland noted five and a half feet on the ground on April 7, 1748.

Big rainstorms and large floods or freshets were often recorded in personal diaries, too. On April 9, 1901, flooding on the Penobscot River damaged many bridges and 6

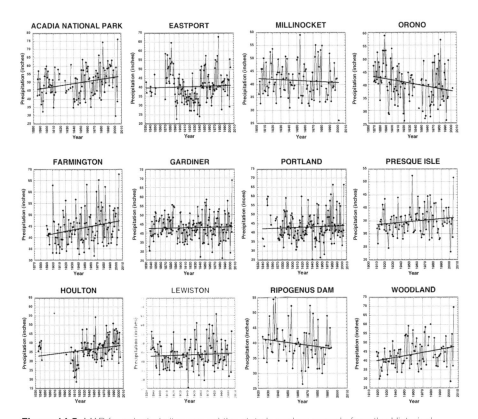

Figure 14.5. MAP for selected sites around the state based on records from the Historical Climatology Network (HCN). These are the raw data with no statistical manipulation. Graphs constructed from data from the National Climatic Data Center. Solid lines indicate the best-fit linear trends to the data.

inches of rain fell in two days at Bemis on Rangeley Lake (Ludlum, 1976). More detailed information comes from accounts of three other big storms in southern Maine. One of these was on October 20, 1785, when two days of hard rain on east-southeast winds dropped up to 9 inches on eastern New England, including southernmost Maine. Both Berwick and Kennebunk reportedly lost nearly every mill and bridge. A second example was the lengthy period of rain from May 13–17, 1814. Damage included the destruction of a bridge over the Mousam River in Kennebunk and damage to many dams and mills. Floodwaters of the Saco River destroyed a bridge in Fryeburg, as well as a bridge farther downstream in Hiram. Damage along the Androscoggin River was equally devastating as 8 sawmills, an aqueduct, and part of the bridge between Topsham and Brunswick were carried away. Similar accounts came from Waterford and Windham (Perley, 2001). Another severe southeast storm began mid-afternoon on April 24, 1827, producing tremendous flooding along many southern Maine streams, including the Cape Neddick, Kennebunk, Saco, Presumpscot, and Androscoggin Rivers. As in the previous examples, flooding from these rains damaged or destroyed many bridges and gristmills in this part of the state. The storm also drove several ships ashore in Portland and many ships in the harbor were damaged due to collisions between vessels that broke free from the wharves (Perley, 2001).

The nor'easter of November 30, 1842 greatly impacted Maine's marine industry. It produced significant snowfall in coastal areas and severe cold, such as in Belfast where the high was 6°F. At sea, several ships were destroyed that had set sail from Maine. The bark *Isadore* left that morning from Kennebunk, heading to New Orleans, but never made it past Cape Neddick, having been driven onto the rocks at Bald Head. The entire crew of 15, all from Kennebunkport, was lost. The schooner *Napoleon* set sail from Calais for New York on November 28 with a cargo of lumber. The ship lost both its masts, capsized, was righted, and then floated helplessly in the Gulf of Maine. It eventually reached a point 40 miles south of Monhegan Island, where the schooner *Echo*, from Thomaston, encountered it. The captain of the *Echo* boarded the *Napoleon* to find that the entire crew had died except the mate, who was severely hypothermic. The same storm also drove the schooner *James Clark* onto Rye Beach, in New Hampshire, following its departure from Portland the day of the storm. Five children and three adults died, primarily from exposure to the cold and waves that battered the ship as it grounded (Perley, 2001).

There are even examples of tornadoes in diaries and newspapers. On June 14, 1892, a tornado in Orono blew down chimneys, uprooted trees, and unroofed buildings. An anemometer in the area recorded 98 mph winds. Other historic tornadoes included the August 12, 1752 storm in Portland that "Blew down houses and barns and everything in its way," as was recorded in the Rev. T. Smith journal. In fact, in 1638 a John Jocelyn recorded one of the earliest major storms in Maine. He recorded that "a fearful storm of wind began to rage, called a hurricane. . . . many trees blown down, ships wrecked."

There are several accounts of what was surely a powerful cold front moving through the state. For example, there are records from Belfast in 1861 on the night of February 7 of a rapid temperature change from 24°F to -32°F by 7:00 on the morning of the 8th. Temperatures on the 8th "warmed" up to -20°F by 4:00 in the afternoon, but that was it (Ludlum, 1968). Another large temperature drop occurred in 1810, as recorded by Professor Cleaveland, of Bowdoin College, Brunswick. He saw a drop from 41°F at noon on January 18 to -10°F at 8:30 on the morning of the 19th (51°F drop overnight). Thermometers in Castine reportedly dropped 44°F in 8 hours with the passage of that same cold front (Ludlum, 1966).

■ CHANGES IN CLIMATE AND ENVIRONMENTAL RECORDS

Changes in certain environmental and biological phenomena over time can also be used to reconstruct past climate changes. This type of information may not be particularly reliable but, in some cases, very useful quantitative information can be garnered. Such information may well support the recorded instrumental data. These records can also be variable as to the type of climatic information they yield. Some may provide records of temperature trends, some may record changes in precipitation, and some may be composite records of multiple factors influencing the environment.

One record that dates back into the 1700s is the timing of past frosts and the length of growing seasons. Baron and Smith (1996) used records from diaries to develop a record of first and last frosts and the resulting growing seasons for Maine's three climatic divisions. The records end in 1947 because after that, the first and last dates with a temperature of 32°F were adopted to indicate the growing season. In coastal areas the length of the growing season averaged 143 days, shorter than the 1971–2000 average of 150 days (Fig. 5.6). Pre–1948 growing seasons in the southern interior were around 125 days—shorter by as many as 15 days than the current season (Fig. 5.6). The pre-1948 growing season in northern Maine was about 120 days, which is actually about the same or even longer than the current 100-120 days (Fig. 5.6). Part of this difference is probably due to methodology differences between past and present guidelines, but it does lend some support to the instrumental records for northern Maine that indicate that part of the state may be cooling slightly.

As I noted earlier, temperature records indicate that Maine winters have been getting warmer. Individuals from the U. S. Geological Survey in Augusta have done many studies of different aspects of Maine's environment that highlight and support this trend in changing winter conditions.

One of the most interesting and longest records measures the times of lake ice-out around the state (Hodgkins et al., 2002). Generally thought to be an indicator of air temperatures in the month or two before ice-out, thus indicating late winter and early spring temperature changes, records were used for 24 lakes in Maine and 5 others in the rest of New England to determine changing temperatures over the last 150 years. Records for Maine lakes begin at various times, with some records, such as for Sebago Lake, starting as early as 1807. Other long records began in the 1830s (Damariscotta and Auburn lakes) and 1840s (Cobbosseecontee and Moosehead). Most of the other records begin in the 1860s to 1880s, with some in the early 1900s to 1920s. Authors of this study have noted possible biases by different observers, the shape of lake, or its north-south position.

At any rate, ice-out has been occurring earlier in all lakes except one over 100 years of record, but that is an expected result. Using Moosehead Lake as representative of lakes in northern and mountainous areas, records indicate a 9-day earlier ice-out since 1850, with most of that change occurring since 1868. There was another period of early ice-out from 1875 to 1900. There is, however, a great deal of variability year-to-year in all records. In southern Maine, ice-out dates are about 16 days earlier now compared to 1850, using Damariscotta Lake as representative of southern and coastal lakes. As with Moosehead Lake, the greatest changes have come since 1868. Although several factors may contribute to ice-out, air temperatures in March and April have the greatest cor-

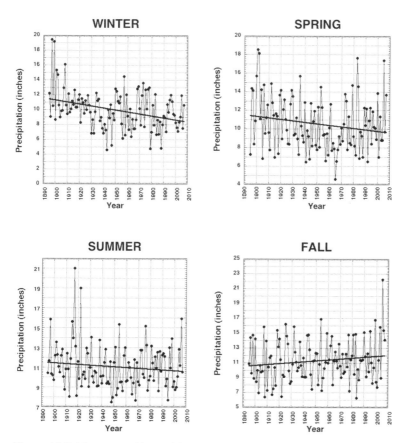

Figure 14.6. Mean statewide precipitation trends for winter, spring, summer, and fall as constructed from data from the National Climatic Data Center. Solid lines indicate the best-fit linear trends to the data.

relation to ice-out. In the northern and mountainous areas, however, ice-out appears to be affected much less by air temperature than in southern and coastal areas, probably because greater snow cover on the lakes provides better insulating and reflecting properties, delaying the eventual ice-out. You could also assume, therefore, that ice-out may be a function of snowfall and late season snow pack in addition to air temperature.

Another study looks at high river flows in Maine over the 20th century. Using data collected from St. John, Fish, Narraguagus, Mattawamkeag, Piscataquis, Sheepscot, Carrabassett, Swift, Little, and Androscoggin Rivers, the study looked at the spring and fall timing of when half of the total volume of stream flow for a given period of time had passed a particular gauging station. The study also looked at the peak flow date. The trends discovered provide an integrated look at both temperature and precipitation conditions around the state, such as seasonal snowfall amounts and the timing of snowfall. Spring runoff will be affected in different ways if the snowfall is evenly distributed throughout the season (when some melting can occur) or if there are more spring storms. Spring and winter temperatures, particularly very high spring temperatures or periods of melt during the winter, will also impact the timing and strength of maximum spring flows. Generally, the largest flows occur in the spring when rain falls on a ripe snow pack or on saturated soils. For instance, over the 60 years from 1930 to 2000, 46% of the total flow of the Swift River occurred in April and May. Large flows in the fall are usually the result of heavy rains that saturate the soil

In general, peak flow on all of Maine's rivers has been occurring earlier in the spring over the 20th century; most of the change occurred from the 1980s to 2000. The long and continuous record from the Piscataquis River—whose flow records begin in 1903—highlights this trend. The timing of peak flow in most of Maine's rivers, especially northern and mountainous rivers, was around May 2 for most of the 20th century, but has begun to occur 1–2 weeks earlier over the last 20 years. The most likely explanation for this trend is the amount and timing of spring snowmelt, indicating that over the last 20 years there has been less snowfall. In addition, warmer Januarys produce more rain events during the month. Furthermore, it is interesting to note that the peak fall flows on the northernmost St. John and Fish rivers have been occurring later.

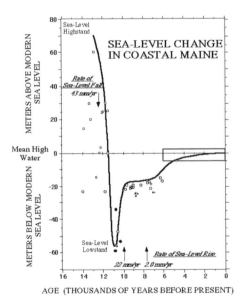

As with many environmental records of this type, however, there is a great deal of year-to-year variability in these records, and the trends identified have been highly influenced by conditions of the last 20 years. Given this relatively short period of rapid change, it is difficult to accurately predict future trends.

River ice thickness provides another example of changing conditions around the state. Once again, the Piscataquis River has been used as a guide for this study as its record is long, extending from 1912 to 2001. This study evaluated ice thickness on February 28 of each year in correlation with such records as winter air and water temperatures and the date of river ice-out. The conclusions from this study show that despite the great amount of annual variability, including years with no river ice, there is an overall trend of thinner ice over time. The total decrease has been about 9 inches (23 cm) from 1912 to 2001—around 0.1 inch/

Figure 14.7. Graph indicating relative sea level in Maine over the last 16,000 years. Figures from Maine Geological Survey publication, Kelley et al., as available at www.maine.gov/doc/nrimc/mgs/explore/marine/facts/sealevel.htm.

year (0.26 cm/year). These numbers are equivalent to about a 45% decrease in ice thickness over the 89 years of record. This trend still holds when you consider the period from 1950 to 1975, when ice thickness increased on the Piscataquis River in conjunction with the cooler temperatures of the 1960s.

The decreasing ice thickness could be a result of an increase in midwinter ice break-up, which is usually associated with rising stream levels after rainfall. Ice-out on the Piscataquis has also been occurring earlier, by 0.21 days/year or about 19 days earlier since 1912.

River temperature data (Huntington et al. 2003) further suggests an overall warming of Maine's climate, as May river temperature records for the Wild River near Gilead for 1966–2001

Figure 14.8. Flooding in Cumberland County caused by the heavy rains during the record setting month of October 2005. Photos courtesy of John Jensenius, Gray NWS.

show an increase in water temperatures at a rate of 0.16°F/year (0.09°C/year). This very high rate of warming, even greater than air-temperature trends, may well be due to the time when record keeping began. This record starts during the cold years of the mid-1960s leading to a very steep change in water temperature over time. If the record went farther back in time, the trend might be lower and more in line with air-temperature trends.

Biological or phenological changes noted over these same time periods also relate well to the physical aspects of our changing environment. For example, photoperiodic (length of day) response of the pitcher plant mosquito (*Wyeomyia smithii*) in Maine is shifting, corresponding to longer growing seasons, as correlated with increasing mean annual temperature. In addition, the timing of salmon migration on the Penobscot River based on fish traps and the timing of adult alewife (herring) migration based on Androscoggin River fish traps have been changing. The study looked at the date of median capture—the date when 50% of the total catch is obtained—from 1983 to 2001 for salmon and from 1986 to 2001 for alewives. In both cases, there has been a trend roughly a day earlier per year over the 15 years or more of record for each species.

Although not direct evidence of local climate change, sea-level changes along the Maine coast are an important result of ongoing, and likely future, global climate changes. It is important to realize that changes in sea level are considered relative because variation along any stretch of coastline depends on both how fast the amount of water in the basins of the world's oceans is changing and how fast the land along the coastline is either rising or sinking. At present, a warmer global climate has resulted in the melting of glaciers around the world and the expansion of the world's oceans. This has resulted in more water being present in ocean basins. The behavior of the land in Maine has been quite variable since the last ice sheets melted away around 14,000 years ago. The response of the earth's crust to this removal of the weight from the ice sheets is to rebound, meaning that at times over the last 14,000 to 5,000 years, much of Maine has been rising. This balance between sea-level rise from melting ice and rising land has produced a relative sea- level curve for the state as shown on Figure 14.7.

In summary, sea level in Maine fell about 1.7 in/yr (14.1 ft/100 yrs) from about 14,000 to 11,000 years ago. Sea level began to rise around 10,000 years ago, starting with an increase of 0.87 in/yr (7.3 ft/100 yrs) and then lesser increases. Tidal gauges now provide records of sea level changes over roughly the last 100 years. These records indicate that sea level in Portland has been rising at an average rate of 0.075 in/yr (0.63 ft/100 yrs) since 1912. The tidal gauge in Eastport indicates a rise in sea level since 1929 of 0.083 in/yr (0.70 ft/100 yrs).

The ramifications of increasing sea-level will need to be taken very seriously as we move ahead with future development of the Maine coast. If global sea level continues to rise as increasing global temperatures cause more glaciers to melt, the potential impact would include the reduction of existing coastal areas and the eventual flooding of homes and communities along the coast, as well as the flooding of existing salt marshes and wetland areas. Wave action from potentially more frequent or more extreme weather events will cause greater damage to existing structures and roads along the shore. Although existing coastal environments may be flooded, new coastal ecosystems will develop farther inland, essentially pushing back the coastline. Regardless of what happens in the future, sea level is changing and both existing environments and human activity along the coast will have to adjust accordingly.

■ THE RECORDS

There seems to be a great deal of interest when weather conditions break a record. The media relishes such newsworthy occurrences and people love to hear about it. Perhaps it is the sense of enduring the very hot or very cold temperatures or wet or dry conditions of a particular year, season, or month. Daily temperature records always make the news, but they can be broken so much easier than longer-term records. This is especially true for precipitation, as a single big storm can easily set a new record.

For the long-term records in Maine temperature, the top ten years are scattered over time since 1895, particularly for the hottest years (Table 14.1). On the other hand, colder years have not been as prevalent throughout the record book. The last cold year that made the top ten was 1989—possibly further evidence that our temperatures have been warming. For monthly and seasonal temperature records, however, the situation is almost reversed (Table 14.2). The hottest months and seasons occurred primarily in the earlier parts of the record—the most recent is the hottest February on record, which occurred in 1981. Despite the lack of recent record-breaking cold years, some of the coldest months on record occurred in the 1990s—January 1994, July 1992 (the summer following the Mt. Pinatubo volcanic eruption), and December 1989. It is interesting to note that yearly temperature records are generally within 10% of the long-term average. The monthly differences from average for precipitation records (Table 14.3) are much greater.

Interestingly, both the wettest and driest years on record have occurred since 2000 (Table 14.3). Some individuals may use this information to support the idea of global warming, as some have argued that the occurrence of extreme events will increase with warmer temperatures. The wettest year on record was 2005 (143% above average; Fig. 14.8.) and the driest year was 2001 (only 69% of average). It is also worth noting that three of the top ten wettest years on record were 1900–1902. Other driest years reflect the major droughts of the mid-1960s (1964 and 1965) and the late 1940s (1949). The mid-1950s also were very dry. Monthly and seasonal precipitation records reflect the wetness of the early 1900s, with the wettest February, March, and April all occurring in the early 1900s. It is interesting, too, that all of the record-setting wet months are more than 200% above average; and, on the other extreme, all of the driest months are only about 30% or less of the average. The record dry October of 1947 was only 10% of an average October. Ultimately, because of their seemingly random occurrence over time, record-setting temperature and precipitation are not reliable for determining future weather trends.

15

WEATHER OF THE FUTURE

The million-dollar question is, of course, what will our weather be like in the future. Unfortunately, there is no simple answer, and the answers that have often been postulated are just possibilities. There is no way to guarantee what the climate will be in the future. There are, however, potential scenarios that have been theorized through a variety of different scientific methods. The most common method to decipher what could happen in the future is the use of global circulation models (GCMs). These computer models take existing conditions then change atmospheric and oceanic conditions to determine how temperature and precipitation patterns may change in the future. Given the increasing levels of carbon dioxide in the atmosphere, one of the most common scenarios run in these models is the effect that higher atmospheric carbon dioxide levels may have on future climatic conditions.

Although these numerical models are very sophisticated, they do not always produce very reliable results when looking at small regions, such as Maine. And when a number of different models are run with the same initial conditions, the results may be very different from model to model. Often the models may agree about whether or not temperatures will rise or precipitation may increase, but the extent of indicated change can vary greatly from one model to another. These models are also very erratic when used to identify future changes in extreme weather events. Just as it is difficult to obtain accurate data when looking at small regions, these models have trouble looking at smaller time events, like hurricanes and other types of major storms.

Despite these shortcomings, computer models provide a potential range of changes that may take place. Consequently, they provide an impetus for planning how to address potential changes to the environment and the overall socioeconomic structure of the region. In the late 1990s and early 2000s, a series of regional climatic assessments were put together across the United States, including an assessment for New England (New England Regional Assessment Group, 2001). In that assessment, several different computer models suggested that temperatures in New England as a whole would continue to rise over the next century, assuming a continued increase of 1% per year in global greenhouse gas concentrations. The New England assessment suggests the possibility of a 2°F increase in minimum annual temperatures over the next 30 years and increases of between 6°F and 10°F in minimum annual temperatures by 2100. Maximum annual temperatures may rise by about 3°F over the next 30 years and between 4°F and 10°F over the next century. This potential magnitude of change, particularly if the 10°F annual changes become reality, is quite dramatic when you consider that annual global temperature differences between almost full glacial conditions and the present is about 10°F. Although such a drastic change has only been modeled, the potential is worth keeping in mind as we move through the 21st century.

At the same time, these same models suggest that annual precipitation across New England will increase over the next century. The models differ quite dramatically in their predictions, but in general, the overall increase across New England is projected to be about 0.5 inch per month to possibly 1.0 inch per month or roughly a 10%–30% increase in annual precipitation over the next 100 years.

These potential changes were modeled for the entire New England region, but, as described in Chapter 14, Maine's climate does not necessarily follow the rest of New England. Whether the same results in future weather conditions would occur in Maine is certainly a subject for debate. Maine could change in the same way as the rest of New England, but at a different rate. This would mean that environmental conditions across the New England region would be characterized by much different gradients than now exist, causing severe changes in overall environmental conditions.

Several potential impacts with increasing temperatures and precipitation have been put forth, not only in the New England Regional Climatic Assessment, but also in other sources and the media. A classic example is that if Maine warms significantly enough, there could be changes in certain types of vegetation. Specifically, there would be a northward migration of maple trees. The models indicate that the prime growing area for many of Maine's tree species would shift anywhere between about 60 and 250 miles. In this scenario, income from sugaring could be greatly reduced and a reduction in maple trees would reduce the vibrancy of the fall foliage season, a rather disappointing possibility for the tourist industry.

Another key impact on the tourist industry with warming would affect the ski and snowmobile industries. Warmer temperatures may lead to less snowfall and possibly a shortened ski and snowmobile season. Warmer conditions, however, do not necessarily mean less snowfall; warmer conditions could still mean that overall temperatures are cold enough that snowfall totals are not so drastically affected. A significant portion of snowfall amount is a function of storm track and the number of nor'easters that impact the state. If storm tracks do not change drastically through the future, it may be that overall snowfall totals will not change either. Unfortunately, however, models are not able to accurately forecast potential changes in single events, so we just do not know the full extent of potential changes.

Another potential problem spot is the rise in water temperature in the Gulf of Maine. Warmer air temperatures could eventually lead to an increase in sea surface temperatures, as well as some increase in temperature with depth. Should this occur, the fisheries of the Gulf of Maine could face some serious changes. Fish that prefer cooler waters may eventually move farther north in the Atlantic Ocean, or possibly farther out to sea, where the deeper waters would remain cooler. This would mean that local fishermen would have to travel much farther to catch the same species they are now able to bring in.

Two general areas of concern related to human health are often listed as potential problems associated with rising temperatures. One is the possible increase in infectious diseases, especially those carried by insects. This situation would be exacerbated with warmer winter conditions as Maine's very cold winters play a major role in reducing the survivability of certain insects. Wetter conditions would also assist in allowing these same insects to thrive across the state. Atmospheric pollution, particularly ozone levels, could also increase with warmer conditions. As summers become warmer, possibly the result of an increase in southerly wind flow, more airborne pollutants and much reduced air quality could become a potential problem. The future is uncertain, but these possibilities could occur and are worth serious thought.

Whatever the future brings, Mainers will have to adjust; proper planning will be important for whatever changes come. Regardless of the nature of how the climate changes, Mainers have demonstrated their resilience in the face of whatever weather nature has thrown at them.

16

WHAT IT ALL MEANS

The weather of Maine is a part of our everyday lives, and regardless of its impact on your personal life, Maine's weather is anything but dull. In fact, if a single word or short phrase were used to characterize Maine's weather, it certainly is dynamic, or diverse, or highly variable. Whatever word or phrase is used, it means that the people of Maine must be prepared for just about anything.

The nature of Maine's weather is best highlighted by the extremes within the state. Conditions range from very cool to cold in The County and the western mountains, to warmer and wetter in Down East, midcoast, and southern coastal regions of the state. Even in coastal regions, however, winter-like conditions can occur any time within at least six months of the year, or more. Northern areas can feel winter-like conditions from late September to early June, a mind-boggling eight months of the year. In fact, the average annual temperature in the Allagash area of northern Maine is 36°F, a mere 4°F above freezing.

Conditions like this have led to the old adage about Maine's weather, that is, it's nine months of winter and three months of poor sledding. Obviously, that is not the case, though in many years there have been very cool summers. On the other hand, it can get fairly hot during a Maine summer, with temperatures occasionally reaching into the 90°Fs and on rare occasions even to the 100°F mark. In fact, the highest temperature ever recorded in Maine is 105°F, and the lowest recorded temperature is -50°F, a range of 155°F.

Precipitation amounts also have a fairly broad range of yearly values, ranging from more than 50 inches along some coastal areas to annual averages in the high 30s in more interior parts of the state. Likewise, seasonal snowfall totals have a wide distribution ranging from more than 50 inches in southernmost coastal areas to more than double that in parts of the northwest hills. This same large spread in snowfall amounts can also be seen in a single snowstorm. In some cases, parts of the state may get no snow or all rain while other parts get dumped on, receiving more than a foot of snow. No matter what type of weather characteristic you look at, conditions can be so very different from one part of the state to the next that it can be difficult to plan an outdoor event.

In addition to Maine's extremes of temperature and precipitation, its weather is also highlighted by so many other weather types. Huge storms test the resolve of people in the state. Perhaps no storm made a greater impact than the Ice Storm of 1998. Roughly four days of freezing rain produced significant ice accumulations on trees and power lines and caused some $200 million in damage around most of the central to southern parts of the state. Blizzards, such as the February 1969 storm that dumped more than 40 inches in many areas of the western mountains and central highlands, or the December 1962 storm that left 30 inches on Bangor, can "shut-down" parts of the state. Winter storms are only part of the story as Maine also can feel the impact of tornadoes and severe thunderstorms, albeit not at the frequency and magnitude of areas like the Great Plains of the United States. Nevertheless, these warm-season storms need to be watched as they can be deadly if you're caught on a hiking trail or, particularly, on the golf course. Hurricanes and tropical storms can also make landfall in the state or, at the least, bring copious amounts of rain. Interactions between tropical systems and extra-tropical storms in the region can lead to some very, very noteworthy storms such as the tremendous coastal damage caused by the All Hallows Eve storm of 1991 (aka "The Perfect Storm") and the record-setting rains of October 1996, that included a single-day total of 11 inches in Portland and storm totals of 19.3 inches in Camp Ellis and Gorham.

If you're paddling a kayak around the coastal islands, you also have to consider the frequent occurrence of fog, which can move in swiftly along the coast. The cool waters of the Gulf of Maine are in sharp contrast to the warm land during the summer, leading to condensation within the air around the coast and frequent summertime fog. In contrast, the relatively warm ocean waters during winter compared to the very cold land and air can produce sea smoke along coastal areas of the state. A heavy fog can make for dangerous conditions in the Gulf of Maine, making it difficult for lobstermen and other fishermen to pursue their living on the open water. There was even an unfortunate fatality in Maine from a dust devil in 2003, a weather event that is not only rare in this part of the United States, but one that rarely leads to injury.

Given this great diversity and variability in weather and climatic conditions across the state, you might give your favorite meteorologist a break since trying to predict accurately the weather across Maine can be so very difficult. Artist dug Nap may have said it best on a t-shirt he designed. It gives the MAINE weather report as "hot & sunny, turning to sleet mid-morning, becoming a blizzard by noon, 6–42 inches, followed by warm, moist, tropical air which will probably bring severe thunderstorms & a flood watch." This plethora of weather epitomizes the range of conditions found in Maine and, consequently, illustrates the hardiness of the people of the state. Our weather is just one reason that Mainers and tourists alike understand why this is "the way life should be" (Fig.16.1).

Figure 16.1. Weather Way, Sebec Lake, National Weather Service Co-op weather station. The name says it all. Photo courtesy of Bill Larrabee.

Appendix: Forecasting in Maine from the Individuals Who Do It

Forecasting for Northern and Eastern Maine
By Hendricus J. Lulofs
Meteorologist-In-Change
NOAA's National Weather Service, Caribou, Maine

As the Meteorologist-in-Charge of the National Weather Service Forecast Office in Caribou, Maine, I lead the team responsible for warnings and forecasts for all of Northern and Eastern Maine as well as the coastal waters along the Downeast Coast. The National Weather Service is part of the National Oceanic and Atmospheric Administration.

Maine experiences a wide variety of significant weather from frequent nor'easters in the winter to spring flooding, to violent thunderstorms in the summer. These threats result in year-round challenges that keep National Weather Service forecasters busy in carrying out their mission of providing weather, hydrologic, climate forecasts and warnings for the protection of life and property and the enhancement of the national economy.

Each of these weather threats brings with its own unique forecast challenges. For example, in the winter many think that forecasting precipitation events for this part of Maine should be easy. It's all about how much snow will fall and where. But more often than not, the area is faced with many precipitation types from each of these storms. Figuring out who will get snow, ice, or rain is a very complicated process. Through computer model guidance provided by NOAA's National Center for Environmental Predication and local National Weather Service forecast expertise the skill in predicting these precipitation types has increased substantially in recent years.

In the spring and summer thunderstorms often produce hail and damaging wind over the region. One of the most underrated killers that accompany these storms is lightning. In Maine, almost every year lightning strikes result in deaths and injuries. The National Weather Service tries to spread the word that no place outside is safe during a thunderstorm!

One of the most difficult high-impact weather scenarios that the National Weather Service in Caribou faces is the forecast of reverse tidal flooding along the Penobscot River. This phenomenon can occur anytime of the year. Reverse tidal flooding occurs when a strong coastal storm moves inland from Penobscot Bay parallel to the Penobscot River. When these storms occur in conjunction with elevated river levels and/or high tide, flooding can occur as water is pushed inland and up the river basin.

Reverse tidal flooding events in Bangor are a grave threat to life and property and have caused millions of dollars of damage in the past. The most significant of these storms occurred on February 2, 1976, when an intense reverse tidal flood developed. Known as the "Groundhog Day" storm, an area of very low pressure skirted just west of the Penobscot River. This low pressure was accompanied by winds of up to 115 miles per hour, waves to 14 feet and a storm surge of 5 feet along the midcoast of Maine. This storm surge was amplified as it was pushed up the Penobscot River nearly 20 miles from the Penobscot Narrows toward downtown Bangor. This wave struck Bangor at 11:15 A.M., just over one hour before high tide. The water was estimated to have risen at a rate of one foot per minute, quickly inundating businesses, roads, and parking areas to a depth of over 12 feet, more than 17 feet above flood stage and 10 feet above the predicted high tide level. More than 200 cars were submerged and many people were trapped in the rising water.

In recent years National Weather Service forecasters in Caribou have on several occasions correctly forecasted the occurrence of reverse tidal flood events, providing advance warnings that helped save life and property. In addition, the Weather Forecast Office in Caribou along with the North East River Forecast Center in Taunton, Massachusetts, have been researching ways to more accurately model and forecast these types of events and their impacts.

While forecasting Maine's weather is never easy, its diverse climate combined with access to the latest technologies available in the science of meteorology makes a career at the National Weather Service quite exciting and rewarding. For more information about the National Weather Service in Caribou visit their Website: www.weather.gov/car.

Forecasting for Western and Southern Maine
By Albert Wheeler
Meteorologist-In-Change
NOAA's National Weather Service, Gray, Maine

As Meteorologist-in-Charge of the National Weather Service in Gray, Maine, weather forecasting in western and southern Maine presents some unique challenges, and is at times a humbling experience.

We provide weather forecasts for the northern end of the Appalachian Mountains, including the summit of Mount Washington, to our west with a height of 6,288 feet. On our eastern side, is the Atlantic Ocean and Gulf of Maine. These geographic features have a profound, and sometimes complex, impact on Maine weather.

The mountains serve as a barrier that can influence the track and intensity of storms. The ocean is a source of moisture for storms, and can at times wreak havoc along the coast with storm tides and pounding surf. The constant interplay between the mountains and the ocean is a major challenge to accurate weather forecasting in Maine, and certainly keeps us on our toes! As Mark Twain once said, "If you don't like the weather in New England, just wait a few minutes." The changeable nature of weather patterns here certainly keeps our job interesting.

The challenging forecast environment can be very rewarding for meteorologists when we successfully provide advance warnings for damaging storms. A good example of this was the "Patriot's Day" storm of April 16, 2007. This storm brought high wind, heavy rainfall, river and coastal flooding that impacted hundreds of thousands of people in western Maine.

Wind gusts of 60 to 80 miles an hour knocked over numerous trees throughout the region and caused widespread and prolonged power outages. Rainfall amounts of up to 7 inches caused major flooding in York County, where homes were ravaged, and roads, bridges and other infrastructure damage was severe. Along the coast, the storm produced damaging storm tides and ocean waves over 30 feet high. The combination of storm tides and battering waves pounded the coast causing major damage.

Damage estimates from the storm were about $30 million. Timely and accurate warnings from National Weather Service meteorologists well in advance of the storm provided time for public officials to prepare by opening storm shelters and positioning their resources most effectively to meet the needs of the community. The advanced forecast also gave power companies time to prepare for the extensive power outages.

Most importantly, our warnings helped people stay out of harm's way during the storm. Our mission at the National Weather Service is to provide timely and accurate warnings and forecasts for the protection of life and property. Like most people, we do not enjoy the severe impacts of major storms, but if we can save even one life through our actions, then all of the effort is very worthwhile.

References Cited

Ackerman, S.A. and J.A, Knox, 2007, Meteorology. Thomson, Brooks/Cole, Belmont, CA, 467 p.

Baron, W.R. and D.C. Smith, D.C., 1996, Growing Season Parameter Reconstructions for New England Using Killing Frost Records, 1697–1947. Maine Agricultural and Forest Experiment Station Bulletin 846, 76 p.

Batchelder, P.D. and M.P. Smith, 2003, Four Short Blasts, The Provincial Press, Portland, ME, 130 p.

DeGaetano, A.T. 2000. Climatic perspective and impacts of the 1998 northern NewYork and New England ice storm. Bulletin of the American Meteorological Society 81: pp. 237–254.

Dudley, R.W. and G.A. Hodgkins, 2002, Trends in streamflow, river ice, and snow pack for coastal river basins in Maine during the 20th century. United States Geological Survey Water-Resources Investigations Report 02-424, 26 p.

Glickman, T.S., 2000. Glossary of Meteorology, 2nd edition. American Meteorological Society, Boston, 855 p.

Hodgkins, G.A., I.C. James II, and T.G. Huntington, 2002, Historical changes in lake ice-out dates as indicators of climate change in New England, 1850–2000, International Journal of Climatology, v. 22, pp. 1819–1827.

Hodgkins, G.A., R.W. Dudley and T.G. Huntington, 2003, Changes in the timing of high river flows in New England over the 20th century, Journal of Hydrology, v. 278, pp. 244–252.

Junger, S., 1998, The Perfect Storm. Harper Paperbacks, New York, 301 p.

Keim, B.D., 1998, Record Precipitation Totals from the Coastal New England Rainstorm of 20-21 October 1996. Bulletin of the American Meteorological Society, v. 79, pp. 1061–1067.

Kelley, J.T., S.M. Dickinson and D. Belknap, Maine's history of sea-level changes, http://www.maine.gov/doc/nrimc/mgs/explore/marine/facts/sealevel.htm

Kocin, P.J., 1983, An analysis of the "Blizzard of '88." Bulletin of the American Meteorological Society, v. 64, pp.1258–1272.

Kocin PJ, Uccellini LW (2004a) Northeast Snowstorms Volume I: Overview. American Meteorological Society, Boston, 296 p.

Kocin PJ, Uccellini LW (2004b) Northeast Snowstorms Volume II: The cases. American Meteorological Society, Boston, 818 p.

Koss, W.J., J.R. Owenby, PM Steurer and D.S. Ezell, 1988, Freeze/Frost Data, Climatography of the U. S., Supplement No. 1, National Climatic Data Center, Ashville, NC, 186 p.

Lombard, P.J., 2004. Drought conditions in Maine, 1999–2002 – A historical perspective. United States Geological Survey Water-Resources Investigations Report 03-4310, 36 p.

Ludlum, D.M., 1966, Early American Winters 1604-1820. American Meteorological Society, Boston, 285 p.

Ludlum, D.M., 1968, Early American Winters II 1821–1870. American Meteorological Society, Boston, 257 p.

Ludlum, D.M., 1976, The Country Journal: New England Weather Book. Houghton Mifflin, Boston, 147 p.

Morrill, R.A., 1977, Maine Coastal Flood of February 2, 1976. United States Geological Survey, Open-File Report 77-533, 29 p.

New England Regional Assessment Group, 2001, Preparing for Changing Climate: The Potential Consequences of Climate Variability and Change. New England Overview. US Global Change Research Program, University of New Hampshire, 96 p.

Perley, S., 2001 (reprinted from 1891), Historic Storms of New England. Commonwealth Editions, Beverly, MA.

Pettigrew, N.R., J. H. Churchill, C.D. Janzen, L.J. Mangum, R.P. Signell, A.C. Thomas, D.W. Townsend, J.P. Wallinga, H. Xue, 2005. The kinematic and hydrographic structure of the Gulf of Maine Coastal Current. Deep Sea Res. II, 52: 2369-2391.

Rao, J., 2002. Moonstruck meteorology: Is it lunacy to think that "Saxby's Gale" could recur this October? Weatherwise, September/October, pp. 23–29.

Ross, T., N. Lott and M. Sittel, 1995, White Christmas? National Climatic Data Center, Technical Report 95-03.

Stommel, H., and E. Stommel, 1983, Volcano Weather. Seven Seas Press, Newport, RI, 177 p.

Watson, B., ed., 1990, New England's Disastrous Weather. Yankee Books, Camden, ME, 228 p.

Zielinski, G.A., 2002, A classification scheme for winter storms in the eastern and central United States with an emphasis on nor'easters. Bulletin of the American Meteorological Society, v. 83, p. 37-51.

Zielinski, G.A., and B. D. Keim, 2003, New England Weather, New England Climate. University Press of New England, Hanover, NH, 276 p.

OTHER SUGGESTED REFERENCES

Aherns, C.D., 1994, Meteorology Today, 5th ed. West Publishing Company, Minneapolis/St. Paul, 591 p.

Balsama, J. and P.R. Chaston, 1997, Weather Basics. Chaston Scientific, Inc., Kearney, MO, 384 p.

Blue Hill Observatory, 1993, The Blizzard of March 1993. Blue Hill Observatory Bulletin, Winter/Spring, v. 11, Blue Hill, ME,16 p.

Bluestein, H.B., 1999, Tornado Alley. Oxford University Press, New York, 180 p.

Bomar, G.W., 1995, Texas Weather, 2nd ed. University of Texas Press, Austin, TX, 275 p.

Cember, R.P. and D.S. Wilks, 1993, Climatological Atlas of Snowfall and Snow Depth for the Northeastern United States and Southeastern Canada. Northeast Regional Climate Center, Publication No. RR 93-1, Cornell University, Ithaca, NY, 19 p. with maps.

Changnon, S.A., 2004, Climate Atlas: Freezing Rain and Ice Storms. Changnon Climatologist, Mahomet, IL, 87 p.

Elsner, J.B., and A.B. Kara, 1999, Hurricanes of the North Atlantic. Oxford University Press, New York, 488 p.

Gelber, B., 1998, Pocono Weather. Uriel Publishing, Stroudsburg, PA, 364 p.

Grazulus, T.P., 2001, The Tornado. Univeristy of Oklahoma Press, Norman, OK, 324 p.

Lamb, H.H., 1995, Climate, History and the Modern World, 2nd ed. Routledge, New York, 433 p.

Ludlum, D.M., 1963, Early American Hurricanes 1492-1870. American Meteorological Society, Boston, 198 p.

Ludlum, D.M., 1970, Early American Tornadoes 1586-1870. American Meteorological Society, Boston, 219 p.

Ludlum, D.M., 1985, The Vermont Weather Book, 2nd ed. Vermont Historical Society, Montpelier, VT, 302 p.

Ludlum, D.M., 1989, The American Weather Book. American Meteorological Society, Boston, 296 p.

Ludlum, D.M.,1998, National Audubon Society Field Guide to Weather. Alfred A. Knopf, NY, 655 p.

Minsinger, W.E., and Orloff, C.T. 1992. Hurricane Bob: August 16-August 20, 1991. Blue Hill Meteorological Observatory, Milton, MA, 80 p.